Drugs as a Social Problem

James D. Wright and Joel A. Devine

Tulane University

Harper Collins College Publishers

Wright/Devine: Drugs as a Social Problem.

ISBN: 0-673-99399-X

Preface and Acknowledgements

Our intention in writing *Drugs as a Social Problem* is to present students with a succinct overview of how America's "drug problem" has come to be defined and treated by government, media, policy-makers, academics, and the general public, that is, to discuss drugs as a *social* issue (as opposed to a medical, personal, or psychological issue). That intention coupled with very tight length restrictions has caused us to omit some material that might otherwise have been included. In particular, we do not discuss the pharmacology or psychobiology of various drugs nor do we spend a lot of time considering proper definitions of terms such as addiction, abuse, withdrawal, psychoactivity, and the like. (There is no professional consensus on the proper definitions of these terms in any case.) Students interested in these issues would be well-served by Akers (1992), Curra (1994: Chs. 10-12), or Lowinson *et al.* (1992), the latter virtually encyclopedic in its coverage. Also, we have focussed our discussion on the most commonly abused substances, specifically, alcohol, marijuana, cocaine, crack cocaine, and heroin; we have said relatively little about the abuse of other legal substances, of prescription drugs, or so-called "designer drugs" such as "ice," PCP, Fantasy, amyl nitrate, "poppers," and on through a long and continually changing list of less commonly used mood-altering substances.

We are pleased to acknowledge the able assistance of Tupper Lampton Allen in doing some of the initial leg work for this book. We are also grateful to Lise Diamond-Devine, Christine Stewart, Joseph Sheley, Derek Wright, and an anonymous reviewer for critical comments and suggestions on earlier drafts, even as we absolve them of any responsibility for the final product. Much of the material contained here was first tried out on students in our course on contemporary American social problems; we are grateful to them for raising the questions that this book tries to answer. Much of our thinking about drugs and related social problems was stimulated while we were involved in research and evaluation in the New Orleans Homeless Substance Abusers Project; we thank the National Institute of Alcohol Abuse and Alcoholism for their gracious and generous support of that project. Finally, we express thanks to our colleagues in the Department of Sociology at Tulane University for creating an intellectual environment where work of this sort is both possible and valued.

i

Table of Contents

One

Drugs: What Is the Problem?

Introduction

Presidents, members of Congress, media commentators, and scholars have all told us that America has a serious drug problem. What are the nature, scope and dimensions of this problem? Has the drug crisis been felt more or less equally throughout society, or are some groups affected more than others? Which groups? In what ways have drugs come to affect society as a whole? And what, if anything, can be done? These and related questions comprise the subject matter of this small book.

It may seem pedantic to begin by asking, "What is the drug problem?" But the answer is not obvious. For example, if we consider the term "drug" in its widest possible meaning, it includes a vast array of substances from aspirin to alcohol to crack cocaine and it becomes obvious that drugs are used casually, thera-peutically, or recreationally by the vast majority of Americans. In fact, the use of mood-altering substances is for all practical purposes a universal human behavior embraced by all known cultures (Weil, 1972). Nearly all of us are "drug users" for some purpose at one or another time.

The near-universal use of drugs makes it essential to distinguish between legitimate drug *use* and destructive drug *abuse*. Everywhere, the use of certain mood-altering substances is both legal and socially sanctioned (or even encouraged) whereas the use of certain other substances is socially disapproved, often strongly. Essential as the distinction may be, however, it is not always a clear one.

To illustrate, consider a product harvested by Colombian peasants, processed, shipped to the United States, and used habitually and even addictively by well more than a hundred million American citizens. The product is coffee and the drug is caffeine, a powerful and addictive stimulant. (The comedian George Carlin once referred to coffee, correctly, as "the low end of the speed

1

spectrum.") Millions of people find it literally impossible to start the day without coffee and habitually consume it throughout their waking hours. Each cup contains about 110 milligrams of pure caffeine--depending on the size of the cup, the type of bean used, the brewing method, and other factors (Kirk-Othmer Encyclopedia of Chemical Technology, 1983: 750-751). Withdrawal from caffeine produces symptoms similar in some respects to those produced by withdrawal from other addictive drugs: headaches, irritability, listlessness, distraction. Yet who would include caffeine addiction as part of America's drug problem?

Consider another product harvested by Colombian peasants, processed, shipped to the United States, but used habitually or addictively by only a few million people, if that. The product is cocaine, also a stimulant, whose smokeable form, crack cocaine, has (or so it is said) swept through the inner cities, leaving a wide swath of human and social destruction in its wake. No one would dispute that the crack epidemic lies at the heart of the American drug problem. But what makes crack cocaine addiction so obviously a problem when caffeine addiction clearly is not?

America as a Drug Culture

America can be fairly called a "drug culture" in the sense that nearly everyone uses drugs of one sort or another. When we are ailing, we expect to be given some drug that will make us feel better. If we have trouble sleeping, we take sleeping medications, whether over-the-counter or prescribed. If we feel anxious, we want anti-anxiety drugs and if we feel depressed we seek anti-depressants. If we want sex without the risk of pregnancy, we take "the pill." Millions of us get "up" with caffeine and come "down" with alcohol. It has even been argued that mood-altering drugs satisfy an *innate* human need to suspend ordinary awareness, a need much like sexual tension that "arises spontaneously from within, builds to a peak, finds relief, and dissipates" (Weil, 1972: 22). The use of drugs to make one feel better or to solve one's problems, whatever they might be, is deeply entrenched in our culture and our expectations.

The distinction between problematic and unproblematic drug use is not just a distinction between legal and illegal substances. In terms of avoidable and thus unnecessary morbidity (illness) and mortality (death), all of the illegally abused drugs *combined* take nowhere near the annual toll that alcohol and nicotine take. Cigarette and alcohol consumption are legal adult behaviors far more conse-quential for the health and well-being of society than heroin, cocaine, or marijuana. Other commonly abused and therefore problematic but legal substances include laxatives (very commonly abused by people with eating disorders), inhalants, and prescription drugs. A particular substance does not have to be illegal to be abused and therefore problematic.

Thus, when we speak of the American drug problem, we must be clear about just what the problem is. Normally, one would not use the phrase "drug problem" to refer to the casual, therapeutic, or recreational use of legal substances in moderation, however problematic the use of these drugs (caffeine, nicotine, alcohol, *et cetera*) might be on other grounds.

The key terms are *legal* and *moderation*. Nearly any legal substance can be used immoderately and become a problem--for specific individuals if not for society at large. Consider the case of alcohol. About three-quarters of U.S. adults consume alcohol at least occasionally (National Institute of Drug Abuse [NIDA], 1991b: 121). In 1990, the average U.S. household spent about $300 on alcoholic beverages (U.S. Bureau of the Census, 1992: 444), roughly equivalent to a bottle or two of good whiskey per month. In fact, more Americans use alcohol than any other drug except caffeine (National Institute on Alcohol Abuse and Alcoholism [NIAAA], 1990: 14).

Alcohol consumption is legal and the production of alcoholic beverages constitutes a significant portion of the American economy. In 1990, alcohol production (not including distribution and sales) was a $20 billion a year industry employing more than 50,000 people with an annual payroll of nearly $2 billion (U.S. Bureau of the Census, 1990: 20H-15); alcohol sales average about $40 billion *per annum*. In moderation, alcohol eases tension, promotes sociability, relieves stress, stimulates the appetite, thins the blood, lengthens life expectancy, and is probably good for one's health (see, e.g., Turner, Bennett, and Hernandez, 1981; Anderson, Casteeli, and Levy, 1987). Practically nothing about the moderate use of alcohol constitutes a "problem."

Still, perhaps a tenth of the U.S. adult population uses alcohol immoderately--has a "drinking problem" even if they are not truly alcoholics (Kinney and Leaton, 1992). Survey data reveal that approximately half the total alcohol is consumed by this 10% who say they drink every day (Fisk, 1984: 5; Winick, 1992). Alcohol is responsible for a high percentage of deaths from heart, liver and other body system failures (Goodwin, 1992), is involved in between half and two-thirds of all homicides (Pernanen, 1991; Murdoch et al., 1990), and is probably involved in an equal or higher number of suicides. About 40% of all motor vehicle fatalities involve a driver who had been drinking (NIAAA, 1987). Alcohol use by pregnant women causes birth defects (Jones et al., 1973); alcohol consumption is responsible for a great deal of morbidity in the population every year. Alcoholics have high rates of separation and divorce and alcohol is implicated in many or most cases of child and spousal abuse (Famularo et al., 1986; Leonard and Jacob, 1988; Norris and Cubbins, 1992). Half or more of the men doing felony time are alcoholic (Collins, 1986; Goodwin et al., 1971; Wright and Rossi, 1986). Alcohol causes people to lose their jobs or to be injured while working and lowers national productivity (Englehart et al., 1992).

Thus, immoderate alcohol use and abuse certainly are part of America's drug problem. In fact, in terms of numbers and total costs, alcohol abuse constitutes the largest single share of the overall drug problem.

Private Troubles vs. Public Issues

It is easy to see that drug use becomes a drug *problem* only when the *conse-quences* become problematic. In turn, a drug problem becomes a *social* problem only when the consequences begin to affect large segments of society and when public action to remedy the problem is deemed both possible and desirable.

It is useful to recall Mills' (1959) distinction between private troubles and public issues. Private troubles threaten individual values and result from unique and limited circumstances. Public issues, in contrast, emerge from general circum-stances, threaten social values, and can only be resolved through collective action. Our focus in this book is not on drug use and abuse as a personal problem; we look beyond the symptomatology of individual users to examine the consequences for the nation as a whole.

4

In order to be precise about what America's drug problem is, we must spell out in detail just what social consequences of drug use we collectively find problematic or objectionable. Setting aside moralistic objections, we can say that drugs are now widely *considered* to be a social problem because:

(1) Large numbers of people now routinely use illicit substances or abuse legal ones on a regular basis; "virtually every corner of American society is influenced by illicit drugs in one way or another" (Staley, 1992: 4). Thus, the demographics, trends, and patterns of drug use are considered in Chapter Two.

(2) Drug use and abuse cost a lot each year, in medical treatment, lost productivity, and increased criminal justice costs. Chapter Three considers various estimates of the costs of America's drug problem.

Large surveys of the American population reveal only very small percentages who use illegal drugs on any regular basis; they also show that illegal drug use has been *declining* for the last decade. In the general (surveyable) population, America's "drug problem" is almost entirely alcohol and tobacco abuse. Likewise, estimates of the costs of the drug problem are too uncertain to sustain useful conclusions. Attention therefore turns to sub-groups where the drug problem is presumably more intense:

(3) Drug use and abuse are often considered a major cause of the decline of cities and the continuing impoverishment of the urban poor. Drug abuse, it is said, makes and keeps people poor and prevents their full participation in the economy and society. Drugs are directly implicated in the continuing decay and disorganization of impoverished neighborhoods in the inner city. Chapter Four takes up the issues of drugs, the cities, and the urban poor.

(4) It is frequently asserted that young people are especially attracted to drugs; drug use is said to destroy motivation, interfere with intellectual and social development, and cause many to drop out of high school, become involved in crime, or behave in other deviant and socially irresponsible or unproductive ways. Various beliefs about addiction and drug use among the young are considered in Chapter Five.

5

(5) Drugs are held responsible for a large share of the American crime problem. Addicts commit crime to support drug habits; the illicit commerce in drugs is an increasingly violent business; the police, the courts, and the prisons have been overwhelmed by the consequences of illegal drug use. Chapter Six takes up the "drugs-crime" connection.

(6) Finally, alcohol and drug abuse corrode the physical and emotional well-being of the American population, a topic considered in Chapter Seven.

Drugs are often thought to cause or worsen most other problems that beset American society: crime and violence, poverty and homelessness, AIDS and ill health, even the high cost of government. Chapter Eight considers whether more and better alcohol and drug treatment is a plausible solution to this growing problem; we conclude that it probably is not. Alternative solutions are considered in the concluding chapter.

Historical and Legal Context

We must stress that drugs are not a new nor a uniquely American problem. The exact origins of today's drug problem are difficult to trace (Inciardi, 1986: 1), but are surely rooted deep in history. Opium is a natural exudate of the poppy plant from which heroin is manufactured and has been recognized as a potent analgesic and euphoria-inducer throughout history. Beer was brewed in ancient Egypt and China, and every civilization has had some sort of alcoholic beverage in common consumption. References to marijuana use appear in early Greek, Hindu, Persian, Arab, and Chinese writings (Inciardi, 1986). When the Spanish *conquistador* Francisco Pizarro began his plunder of Incan civilization in 1513, he discovered that chewing coca leaves (from which cocaine is derived) had been part of Incan custom and mythology for centuries.

Drug use was also common in America until the 1900s. In the 1800s, America was a "dope fiend's paradise" (Brecher, 1972:3) where opium, heroin, morphine and their derivatives were as accessible as aspirin is today. Opium "dens" were common; also, many 19th century nostrums contained doses of opiates that would be considered shocking and dangerous today. The term *Coca*-Cola leaves no doubt about the product's original narcotic content.

6

So how did we evolve from a nation where manufacturers could routinely add narcotic substances to common consumer goods to a nation where the mere possession of small quantities of the same substances results in stiff, mandatory prison sentences?

The U.S. Constitution granted limited powers to the federal government and reserved all other powers to the several states, especially police powers. Thus, early 20th century efforts by the federal government to regulate domestic drug use were declared unconstitutional (Bureau of Justice Statistics [BJS], 1992: 76). Consequently, the first federal drug control initiatives were limited by Constitutional interpretation to tactics involving only taxes and treaties.

By 1900, it was believed that there were 250,000 habitual users of narcotics in the country, enough to motivate the states to enact anti-drug legislation. Most of these efforts focussed on morphine and cocaine, the principal drugs of abuse (other than alcohol) at that time. The first federal narcotics regulations did not target the domestic drug problem directly: one banned the importation of opium by Chinese nationals in 1887 and another attempted to regulate opium smoking in the Philippines (then a U.S. colony) in 1905 (BJS, 1992: 80). Domestic regulation of narcotics by the federal government began in 1906, when Congress enacted the first Pure Food and Drug Act (Brecher, 1972:47). The Act only required that medicinal products containing opiates and other specified drugs have labels that correctly identified these ingredients; actual use of narcotics was not restricted.

Regulatory attitudes changed dramatically with the 1914 Harrison Narcotics Act, to which current attitudes and policy towards drugs can be traced. The Harrison Act and its subsequent interpretation by the Supreme Court severed the supply of legal opiates available to addicts (Brecher, 1972:47). The Act mandated that all involved in the importation, manufacture, production, compounding, sale, dispensing or distribution of cocaine and opiate drugs or any product containing these drugs must register with the Treasury Department, record all transactions involving these substances, and pay special taxes (Inciardi, 1986: 14-15). The intent of this legislation was to establish a revenue code that would exert public control over narcotics, not to penalize the existing addict population. Still, the Act soon came to be used for both punitive and regulatory purposes.

The Harrison Act allowed physicians to prescribe, administer, or dispense narcotics "in the course of professional practice" and for "legitimate medical purposes" (Inciardi, 1986: 15). What qualified as a "legitimate" medical purpose, however, was ambiguous. The use of opiates to relieve pain was certainly legitimate (and remains so today). But what of the use of narcotics to "relieve" narcotic addiction itself? The criminal justice system interpreted the Act to mean that physicians could not prescribe narcotics to addicts just to maintain them in their addiction, and the courts agreed (Brecher, 1972: 49). According to the thinking of the times, addiction was a behavioral aberration, not a "disease," and so prescribing narcotics for addicts *just because they were addicts* was considered outside the bounds of "professional practice" and thus illegal. What began as concern with orderly marketing of narcotics quickly became a prohibition against supplying addicts with narcotics even via a prescription; for the first time, narcotic addiction itself became a crime.

Today, addiction is almost universally considered to be a disease. (We consider the "disease" theory in Chapter 8.) Nevertheless, the legacy of the Harrison Act remains, especially in the definition of narcotics usage as a crime in itself and the consequent forcing of addicts out of legitimate society and into the underworld. The Harrison Act and its adjudicated broad federal police powers endured as the foundation of narcotics regulation in the U.S. for the next 50 years (BJS, 1992: 76). The numerous amendments to the Harrison Act were consolidated in the Comprehensive Drug Abuse Prevention and Control Act of 1970, especially in Title II (the Controlled Substances Act) and Title III (the Controlled Substances Import and Export Act), the current legal authority for nearly all federal drug control measures (BJS, 1992: 77).

The Harrison Act and its moralistic antipathy towards drug use are usually considered the nation's first "war on drugs." Prohibition was part of this initial effort. Prohibition was eventually repealed, but the Harrison Act was not. The nation's second "war on drugs" was launched early in the Nixon administration; Nixon declared that drugs were "Public Enemy Number One" and called for a "total offensive." The Comprehensive Drug Abuse Prevention and Control Act of 1970 was part of this offensive.

The "total offensive" lost momentum in the 1970s when eleven states decriminalized marijuana, with the support of such mainstream organizations as the American Medical Association, the American Bar Association, the American Public Health Association, the National Council of Churches, and the National Commission on Marijuana and Drug Abuse. But the tide turned again during Ronald Reagan's presidency when he pledged "to do whatever is necessary to end the drug menace" and declared yet a third "war on drugs" on October 14, 1982.

The weapons in our current war on drugs are breath-taking in scope and expense. On the supply side are large-scale crop eradication and crop substitution programs in the producer countries, interdiction of drugs on the high seas and at our borders, aggressive prosecution of drug trafficking and money laundering conspiracies, some involving foreign heads of state (for example, Panama's Manuel Noriega), and seizure of assets derived from drug trafficking. On the demand side, the Anti-Drug Abuse Act of 1988 placed heavy emphasis on "user accountability." The 1988 Act imposed civil fines without trial of up to $10,000 for the possession of illegal drugs even in quantities appropriate only for personal use. It also permitted federal district judges to sanction drug possessors by disqualifying them from selected federal benefits for up to one year. The 1988 Act also established a "drug czar" to oversee anti-drug activities. Successive initiatives and acts have mobilized many federal agencies on both the domestic and international fronts; many states and local jurisdictions have responded with severe mandatory sentences for drug sales, possession, and use. Total federal spending in the war on drugs increased from about $1 billion per year in the early 1980s to more than $9 billion in the late 1980s (Wisotsky, 1990) and has since risen to about $12 billion (Horgan, 1993). President Clinton has promised to maintain or even strengthen federal initiatives in this area.

What has been the effect of our current "war on drugs"? We argue in Chapter 9 that it has been a disaster. Hysteria about drug use has been commonplace throughout the 20th century. At present, crack cocaine causes the most concern, but less than a decade ago, it was heroin, and before that marijuana, and alcohol (Prohibition), and opium. What was said about the "drug problem" in earlier eras is being said again today. U.S. history since the Harrison Act has been one long, expensive experiment to determine whether "getting tough" on drugs is a workable drug policy. The results are in. The answer is no.

Summary

Although drug use and abuse are clearly problems in contemporary American society, some caution must be exercised in stating just what the drug problem is. The next several chapters review evidence on the scope and consequences of America's drug problem; the final two chapters consider evidence on possible solutions. We acknowledge the problematic aspects of drug use, but caution is necessary because exaggeration, misrepresentation, and outright misstatement are not uncommon. Our aim is to make students more intelligent consumers of information about the drug problem and to elevate the debate over drug policy to a more critical and empirical plane. And while we have our own ideas about what strategies will work and what ones will fail, any attitude about American drug policy should be rooted in reason and evidence, not in emotion or ideological passions. As we shall see, this standard is routinely violated by many commentators on America's drug problem.

Two

Drugs: Demographics, Trends, and Patterns of Use

Introduction

How many people of what sorts use which kinds of drugs? Are the numbers increasing, decreasing, or holding constant? Is the drug problem general throughout society or restricted to small, atypical subgroups?

There is no lack of assertions that America's drug problem has touched a vast segment of society. Consider the following passage (taken from the Robert Wood Johnson Foundation [RWJF] publication, *Substance Abuse*):

"It is the worst of plagues. It knows no season and no boundaries. No mosquito will ever be identified, no microbe isolated, no vaccine invented to end its reign. It is a pestilence with all the classic trappings of social disruption, suffering, and death--and one terrible, defining difference: we invite it to kill and maim and diminish us. (...) And because its vector is pleasure and its mask is time, we have not even recognized its horror fully enough to grant it a name worthy of its grisly power. How inadequate it is to call this peerless filler of graves and plunderer of nations by so pallid a name as *substance abuse*" (RWJF, 1992: 2).

In the face of such rhetorical flourish, it may seem insensitive to ask what the evidence shows about substance abuse in the general population. But ask we must. The methods of epidemiology are useful in giving some sense of the dimensions of the plague that allegedly besets us. Looking at drug use patterns over time tells us whether the problem is waxing or waning. Likewise, looking at variables of person tells us whether drug use patterns are different among varying ages, genders, races, and socio-economic statuses. Variables of place tell us whether the drug problem varies by geography, i.e., by region or city size. The best evidence is provided by ongoing, large-scale surveys, especially the National Household Surveys on Drug Abuse (NHSDA) conducted by NIDA.

The NHSDA has been administered 12 times from 1972 to the present, so a long time-series of data is available. The goal of these surveys is to measure the prevalence and correlates of drug use and abuse. All the NHSDA surveys ask about both lifetime use (i.e., *any* use of a particular substance over the entire lifetime), use in the previous year, and use in the past thirty days (i.e., current use of a particular substance). Thus, the data allow us to distinguish between historical *versus* currently active use patterns.

Strengths and Weaknesses of the NHSDA Surveys

Sample surveys such as NHSDA are appropriate for estimating current and lifetime drug usage rates in the population at large because, first, they are based on national probability samples and therefore generalize statistically to the population in which we are interested, and second, because they measure usage that would not ordinarily come to the attention of the authorities and would otherwise not be included. Thus, survey data are more complete than official statistics available from police, hospitals, or other records. The situation is analogous to the measurement of the crime rate. Most crime is never reported to the police and therefore not reflected in "official" crime statistics; in order to obtain a complete picture, it is necessary to survey samples of people about their criminal victimization. Likewise with drug use.

The NHSDA surveys are very high quality. The sample sizes are large (more than 30,000 respondents), the response rates are acceptable, and the surveys are done with face-to-face interviews. These surveys obtain usage data on all persons within sampled households age 12 and above.

That said, the NHSDA studies are not without problems. First, the data are based on self-reports, so their value depends on accurate and truthful responding. Studies have established that self-report data on drug use are generally valid; the NHSDA survey procedures have been designed specifically to encourage honesty and accurate recall. Still, it is possible that some people under-report their actual drug use (and that others over-report, although this is a less serious concern). A cautious analyst would therefore take the NHSDA estimates of usage rates as lower-boundary estimates, not as "best guesses."

Second, the NHSDA surveys are cross-sectional, not longitudinal. A new sample is drawn each year (vs. reinterviewing the same people year after year, as in a longitudinal or panel survey). The surveys provide a series of annual snapshots: they show aggregate trends across time, not how individual use patterns may vary over time.

Third and most seriously, the target population of the survey is the population of *households* in the 48 coterminous states. By design, this excludes Alaska and Hawaii and also all persons who do not reside in households. The latter consists of persons residing in group quarters (for example, military installations, college dormitories, and group homes), in institutions (for example, prisons, nursing homes, and treatment centers), and persons with no permanent household residence (homeless people and residents of single-room occupancy hotels).

It is estimated that these sample exclusions represent less than 2% of the total U.S. population and so the resulting bias in the data is not large in sheer numerical terms. On the other hand, rates of drug abuse are almost certainly much higher than average among many of these groups: prisoners (considered in Chapter 6), the homeless, and people in alcohol and drug treatment centers (taken up in Chapter 8). If drug use patterns among these excluded groups differ sharply from those of the household population, as they certainly do, then the NHSDA estimates will be correspondingly inaccurate. It is a fair generalization that America's drug problem tends to be strongly concentrated among the very groups that the NHSDA sample design excludes.

In general, the inaccuracy will be negligible for common drugs such as alcohol, but it may be considerably more serious for drugs such as heroin (NIDA, 1991a: 5). Suppose that in the surveyed household population, one person in five hundred has used heroin in the previous month. But suppose that among the excluded 2% of the population one person in ten has used heroin in the previous month. Ten percent of 2% is 0.2% so the "correct" estimate of heroin use is 0.4%, not 0.2%, a difference of a factor of two. It is easy to see that if usage of a particular drug is extremely rare among the household population but very common among the excluded population, the NHSDA estimates can be very wide of the mark.

13

Finally, all surveys and the U.S. Census under-represent young, non-white, poor inner-city residents, another group in which drug use is more widespread than among the U.S. population as a whole (see Chapter 4). This group is under-represented because members are relatively difficult to locate and interview. The under-representation of such persons in all surveys means that caution must be exercised in using NHSDA data to estimate the true rate at which drugs such as heroin or crack cocaine are used and abused.

General Use Patterns

While much attention has been focussed on hard drugs, it is worth emphasizing that the NHSDA surveys and other data sources have repeatedly documented that alcohol and marijuana use is far more common among people of all ages, genders, races, etc. Not surprising, the more socially disapproved a given substance is, the less likely people are to consume it (Akers, 1992: 49).

Table 2.1 shows aggregate use patterns for drugs of various sorts as of the 1991 NHSDA survey. (Only preliminary results from the 1992 survey are available.) Alcohol is the most widely used substance on the list by a considerable margin. Eighty-five percent of the U.S. population have used alcohol at some time and half used alcohol in the previous month. Next are cigarettes, now smoked by a bit more than a quarter of the population, and then marijuana, used at least once by a third of the U.S. population. Use of *any* illicit substance in the past month is reported by 6.2% of the population, mostly marijuana (4.8%). Current use of any illicit substance other than marijuana is reported by fewer than 1%.

Overall patterns of use do not correspond one to one with the extent to which any particular substance can be considered part of America's drug problem; factors other than the sheer number of users must also be taken into account. Still, the findings in Table 2.1 suggest, at minimum, that there is not one drug "problem" but rather two. The first is the routine, habitual use of drugs such as alcohol and nicotine by very large segments of the U.S. population; the second is the habitual use of drugs such as crack, heroin, or hallucinogens by very small segments. For all the anxious alarm that hard drug usage arouses, one is surprised by how few people currently use any of these substances.

Table 2.1: Aggregate Patterns of Drug Use, 1991

Percentage of the total U.S. population who have:

Substance	Ever Used	Used in Past Month
Any illicit drug	37.1	6.2
Marijuana	33.4	4.8
Cocaine	11.7	0.9
Crack	1.0	0.2
Inhalants	5.6	0.6
Hallucinogens	8.2	0.3
Any psychotherapeutic drug	12.6	1.5
Stimulants	7.0	0.3
Sedatives	4.3	0.4
Tranquilizers	5.6	0.4
Alcohol	84.7	50.9
Cigarettes	72.7	27.0
PCP	3.6	--*
Heroin	1.4	--*

Source: NIDA, *NHSDA: Population Estimates, 1991.*
*Use in the past month is too infrequent to measure reliably.

Time

The two-decade trend is also surprising. Contrary to conventional wisdom, the NHSDA data indicate that alcohol and illicit drug use rates have *declined* since the late 1970s and early 1980s (NIDA, 1991a: 13). (These data are summarized in the four figures at the end of this chapter.) By the NHSDA standard, illicit drug use includes any non-medical use of marijuana or hashish, cocaine, crack, inhalants, hallucinogens, heroin, or psychotherapeutics. The surveys show that usage increased regularly throughout the 1970s, peaked between 1979 and 1982, and has been declining since. Comparisons of the 1988 and 1991 surveys show that usage has continued to decline (or has remained stable) for the population as a whole and among all age groups. For all the present day hysteria over drugs, *illicit drug use has actually been dropping for the past decade.*

There is some variation on the theme. Data from the University of Michigan in 1992 revealed slight increases in marijuana and LSD use among young adults, reversing a twelve-year downward trend (Rovner, 1993); the study also suggested a small increase in LSD use among high school students. Even in the NHSDA data, there are always small upward blips for some substances among some subgroups in some years. Whether these are evidence of new trends, temporary aberrations, or normal sampling fluctuations cannot be determined until more data are in.

Person

Patterns of drug use by age show that the downward trend is quite general. We focus on use patterns among three groups: teens (ages 12 to 17), young adults (ages 18 to 25), and adults (ages 26 and over).

Among teens, lifetime use of any illicit substance declined from 34.3% in 1979 to 24.7% in 1988 to 20.1% in 1991 (NIDA, 1991b: 19-20). Thus, in a bit more than a decade, the drug-abusive teen-age population has declined from one in three to one in five. Current use (in the past month) showed an equivalent decline from 17.6% in 1979 to 9.2% in 1988 and 6.8% in 1991. Thus, illicit drug use among teenagers is at an all-time low.

Among young adults (18 to 25), the prevalence of drug use is higher but has followed the same general trend. Between 1979 and 1988, lifetime usage of any illicit drug declined from 70% to 59% (NIDA, 1991a: 21) and use over the past month dropped from 37% to 18%. Here too, the 1991 data reveal the downward trend, lifetime usage dropping to 55% and current use declining to 15%.

Trends among adults are more complicated owing to the maturation of the "drug culture" of the 1960s and early 1970s. Among adults, measured lifetime use has been increasing: from 23% in 1979 to 34% in 1988 and 35% in 1991. This gradual increase is due to the aging of cohorts with high rates of prior drug use rather than an increase in use by middle-aged and older adults (NIDA, 1991a:

16

15). Few persons begin drug use after their mid-twenties, and as a matter of fact, people tend to stop using drugs as they get older (Akers, 1992:49). Current use patterns show the same downward trend: in 1979, 6.5% of all adults had used illicit drugs at least once in the month prior to the survey; in 1988, 4.9%; and in 1991, 4.6%. Illicit drug use is most common among persons aged 18 to 25, followed by teens aged 12 to 17. In general, drug use and experimentation are infatuations of the young and something most people grow out of as they mature. We return to the point in Chapter 5.

The downward trend is also evident for alcohol. NHSDA lifetime and 30-day prevalence rates of alcohol use increased from 1974 to 1979 and generally declined thereafter, reaching an all-time low in 1991 (see, e.g., U.S. Bureau of the Census, 1992: 127). Based on annual per capita consumption, NIAAA (1990: 14) concludes that alcohol consumption has steadily declined since 1981 because of increased public awareness of the risks associated with drinking. Another possible factor may be demographic; alcohol consumption has always been low among those over 60, who are an increasing proportion of the population. Also, social acceptability of heavy drinking has declined in the past decade and this may also be a factor in the trend.

Consumer preference has shifted from hard liquor towards beverages with lower alcoholic content. Wine coolers were first introduced into the market in 1982 or 1983 and by 1986 accounted for one-fourth of total wine consumption (NIAAA, 1990: 14). "Light" beer has also come to command a large share of the market. Drinking less alcohol is part of a "health and fitness" movement that has also resulted in less smoking, increased attention to nutrition and exercise, etc.

The downward trend in alcohol consumption is evident in all age cohorts. Among teens in 1974, 54% had used alcohol at least once. Lifetime use among teens peaked in 1979 at 71% and has declined since, standing at 46% in 1991 (NIDA, 1991a; 1991b). Use in the previous month also peaked among teens in 1979 at 37% and has fallen off to 20% (NIDA, 1991b: 85). The prevalence of alcohol use is markedly higher among those aged 18 to 25 but follows the same pattern. Lifetime use among young adults peaked in 1979 at 95% and has declined (although very modestly) to the 1991 rate of 90%. In 1979, 76% of young adults had used alcohol in the previous month; in 1991, the figure had

17

fallen to about 64%. Finally, among persons 26 and older, lifetime use rates reached a high of 92% in 1979 and have since declined modestly to 89%; use in the past month declined in the same period from 61% to 52% (NIDA, 1991a: 15, 22). While nearly every adult has used alcohol at some time, current usage among all ages is now at its lowest level since NHSDA began monitoring.

Gender differences are small and worth only a brief note. Males are somewhat more likely than females to have used illicit substances (41% to 34%) and alcohol (89% to 81%). The "gender gap" in current illicit drug use is even smaller (8% to 5%) but the difference in current alcohol use is somewhat larger (58% of males have used alcohol in the previous month *versus* 44% of females). There are also small gender differences in what kinds of illicit drugs people use. (All data are for 1991; see NIDA, 1991a.)

Racial differences in use patterns are also generally modest. In the 1991 NHSDA survey, blacks (16%) were somewhat more likely than whites (12%) or Hispanics (12%) to have used any illicit drug within the past year and likewise within the past month (9.4%, 6.4%, and 5.8% for blacks, Hispanics, and whites respectively) (NIDA, 1991b: 20-21). These differences are obviously small. Larger differences are obtained for specific kinds of drugs. In 1991, blacks were more likely than whites or Hispanics to use marijuana, cocaine, and crack; whites were more likely than blacks or Hispanics to use hallucinogens, stimulants, and alcohol; and Hispanics were more likely than blacks or whites to use heroin and PCP.

Given current concerns about the "crack epidemic" and the racial stereotyping in such discussions, the racial and ethnic differences in crack cocaine use merit additional discussion. In the 1988 NHSDA survey, prevalence rates for lifetime use of crack cocaine were twice as high among blacks and Hispanics as among whites. Do these differences reflect race-specific personal factors, as commonly assumed, or do they reflect larger community-level or macro-social factors with which race and ethnicity happen to be correlated?

Reanalysis of the 1988 NHSDA data holding a range of neighborhood variables constant showed no significant residual association between race or ethnicity and crack cocaine usage (Lillie-Blanton *et al.*, 1993). The initial zero-order effects

18

for age and gender remained (men and younger persons are more likely to have used crack than women and middle-aged and older persons), but not those for ethnicity and race. Thus, the apparent effect of race on crack use is an artifact of neighborhood or macro-social factors; "given similar social conditions, crack cocaine smoking does not depend strongly on race *per se*" (1993: 996).

Although one cannot state specifically what the risk factors are that generate high rates of crack abuse, a number of possibilities come to mind: availability of drugs, poverty, unemployment, high morbidity and mortality, access to resources, and degree of contact with the criminal justice system. Race and ethnicity are, of course, strongly associated with all of these. Without attention to these larger social-structural determinants, simple comparisons among blacks, Hispanics, and whites can be dangerously misleading. The findings do not belie the zero-order correlations between race and drug use; they show, rather, that these simple correlations "may lead to misunderstanding about the role of race or ethnicity in the epidemiology of crack use. Shallow and possibly prejudiced misconceptions may be fostered" (1993: 996).

How does drug use vary by socio-economic status? The NHSDA surveys are not ideal for answering this question because the only available indicators of socio-economic status are education and employment. Moreover, these measures are only available for persons age 18 and over. In 1990 (the last year in which results by education and employment status were published), annual usage rates of any illicit substance increased from 11% among those with less than a high school education to 14% among high school graduates and to 16% among those with some college, within a downturn to 12% among college graduates (NIDA, 1991a: 32). Thus, there is a slight tendency for illicit drug usage to increase with education up through some years of college and then to decline, but differences by education are relatively minor. The same general patterns also emerge for usage in the last month or usage over the lifetime, although minor variations surface when looking at specific illicit drugs. So far as alcohol is concerned, the basic pattern is clear: use increases with education. Thus, in 1990, 53% of those with some high school education, 68% of high school graduates, 80% of those with some college, and 79% of college graduates drank alcohol at least once within the past year (NIDA, 1991a: 89).

19

Also contrary to conventional wisdom, no meaningful differences in drug use among young people were found between school-enrolled and high school graduate populations versus school drop-outs. However, results from the 1990 NHSDA survey provide some evidence that the expected differences in marijuana and cocaine use between these groups may emerge later--after the age of 25.

Differences in drug use by employment status are rather sharper. Among employed persons in 1990, about 15% reported some use of illicit drugs within the past year; among unemployed persons, the figure was 26%. (Among those not in the labor force, mostly housewives and retired persons, the rate of illicit drug use was only 6%). The higher rate among the unemployed also holds up when looking specifically at marijuana, cocaine, crack, and hallucinogens. Alcohol use, however, shows a different pattern. Overall, 78% of full-time workers, 76% of part-time workers, 65% of the unemployed, and 51% of those not in the labor force drank alcohol on one or more occasions within the previous year (NIDA, 1991a: 89). Thus, employed people are more likely to use alcohol than the unemployed; the reverse is true for illicit substances.

Concerning lifetime use patterns, the unemployed show the highest use rates for cocaine, crack, inhalants, hallucinogens, PCP, heroin, stimulants, and tranquilizers, whereas employed persons show the highest use rates for marijuana, sedatives, and alcohol. Although these are the general patterns, none of these drug-specific differences in use rates is especially large.

Place

How do various usage rates correlate with region or city size? In general, illicit drug use is slightly higher in the west but the difference is small. Usage rates in the last year were 16% in the western states, 14% in the midwestern states, and 12% in the eastern and southern states (NIDA, 1991a: 32). Results for specific drugs tend to mirror these aggregate patterns; and likewise the results for last-month and lifetime usage. Again, the pattern for alcohol consumption is somewhat different, with last-year usage ranging from 74% in the northeast to 56% in the south.

We have come to think of the "drug problem" as largely an urban problem; however, use of illicit drugs is only slightly correlated with city size in the NHSDA data. Among residents of large cities, 15% reported some use of illicit drugs in the previous year; the rate for residents of small metropolitan areas was 13% and the rate for residents of non-metropolitan areas (small towns and rural areas) was 11%. Illicit drug use is therefore slightly higher in the large urban areas than elsewhere, but the differences are very small. The same pattern is observed for each specific illicit drug and for lifetime as well as last-year use.

Summary

Data generally do *not* support the image of the drug problem as "Public Enemy Number One." Excepting legal substances, usage rates are very low and have been declining since the early 1980s. Most illicit substance use involves marijuana, currently used by about 5% of the population; "harder" illicit drugs such as heroin or crack are currently used by only fractions of a percent.

Expected social correlates of illicit drug use also fail to materialize. There is some evidence that younger people are more likely to experiment with drugs but the general downward trend is observed among all ages; and there is considerable evidence people grow out of drug use as they age. Differences in illicit drug use associated with variables such as gender, race, education, or city size are also consistently small. The general patterns of use and the decade-long downward trend do *not* suggest that America has a terribly serious drug problem (excepting, of course, the continuing use and abuse of alcohol and tobacco by very large percentages of the population).

On the other hand, small numbers can add up to big problems and it would be misleading not to acknowledge that when the percentages are converted to absolute numbers, the drug problem looms larger. Only 0.2% of the U.S. population admits to having used crack cocaine in the last month. But multiplied by the number of people age 12 and over, that small percentage turns into hundreds of thousands of crack users. (The most recent data indicate that about 850,000 people use crack cocaine at least weekly.) It is nearly certain that these hundreds of thousands of chronic crack users do social harm in vast disproportion to their numbers. So it is not quite right to conclude that there is no drug problem just because the large majority do not use or abuse drugs or because the overall use trend is downward. The right conclusion, rather, is that America's illicit drug problem is highly concentrated among a very small fraction of the total population.

There is also good reason to believe that the "small fraction" in question is comprised disproportionally of those very groups excluded from the NHSDA surveys and therefore not reflected in the aggregate data reviewed in this chapter. There are now about one million persons, most of them young males, currently incarcerated in the nation's prisons and jails among whom rates of alcohol and drug use are exceptionally high--on the order of three out of four; and the consequences of alcohol and drug abuse in this population include a continuing degradation of the quality of urban life. There are also about a million homeless people in the United States on any given day (most of them also young males) and at least half are substance-abusive (Wright and Weber, 1987). They too have contributed a disproportionate share to our current social woes. The correct conclusion, therefore, is that America does not have much of a drug problem *among the surveyable portion of the population*. This is not the same as concluding that there is no drug problem at all, only that the evidence for the problem is not to be found in household surveys.

Figure 1

Any Illicit Drug

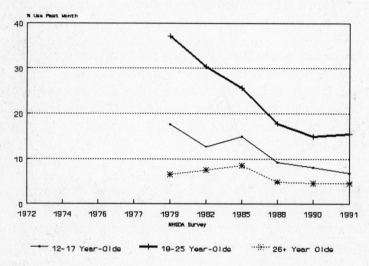

- 12-17 Year-Olds
- 18-25 Year-Olds
- 26+ Year Olds

Figure 2

Marijuana & Hashish

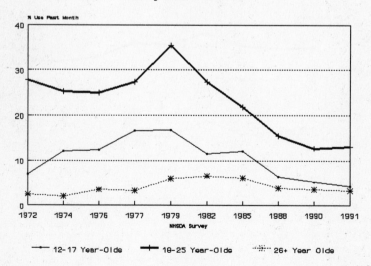

- 12-17 Year-Olds
- 18-25 Year-Olds
- 26+ Year Olds

23

Figure 3

Cocaine

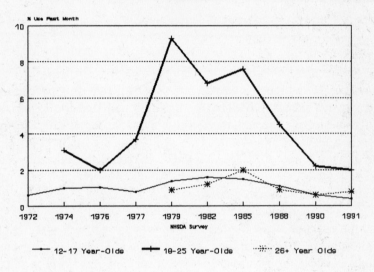

Figure 4

Alcohol

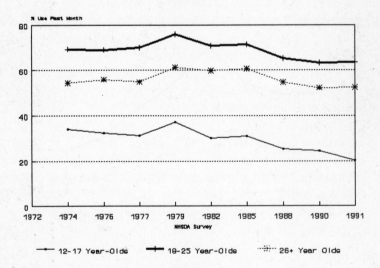

Three

Drugs and Economics

Introduction

If we are unable to find much evidence of a serious illegal drug problem in large household surveys such as NHSDA, perhaps we will find the evidence in the economic costs of drug use and abuse to the nation at large. As we suggested in Chapter 1, a leading objection to drug use is that it costs us a lot of money that could be spent on other needs if the drug problem somehow magically disappeared. So what, then, are the costs of America's drug problem? Are there any associated benefits that need to be taken into account?

Estimating the economic costs of the drug problem is no easy task. Analyzing the available studies shows that hard, reliable data are scarce. Uncertainties in the estimates are so large that nearly any conclusion about costs is defendable, including that drug use and abuse provide substantial economic benefits.

Some of the costs are relatively straightforward and easily estimated. For example, annual expenditures on the War on Drugs are $12 billion. But even this proves more complicated on closer inspection. This $12 billion provides employment for tens of thousands of federal employees who might otherwise be unemployed. Other costs are even more subtle. How does one estimate the economic value of lost productivity from workers whose efficiency is impaired by their hangovers? The value of property stolen by drug addicts to support their addictions? The economic losses incurred when people lose their jobs or are made homeless by chronic alcohol or drug abuse?

Another complication lies in distinguishing between the costs of drug use and abuse *per se* and the costs of our efforts to regulate drugs. The annual outlay for the War on Drugs is not a cost of drug abuse but the cost of our effort to prevent drug abuse. We could freely choose not to incur the cost; reducing or eliminating this annual cost does not require behavioral change on the part of a single addict or drug consumer. In contrast, the cost incurred when drug-

25

impaired drivers require expensive hospital treatment is a cost of drug use *per se*. We cannot just choose not to spend the money; reducing or eliminating this cost requires behavioral change among drug consumers. Much of what is considered to be a cost of drug abuse is in reality the cost of attempting to regulate (or treat) drug abuse, a point to which we return in Chapter 9.

Finally, we should not let our animosity towards drugs and drug abusers blind us to possible economic benefits that result from the "drug problem." The "drug problem" creates a great deal of direct employment in trying to fight it. Drug addiction creates jobs and middle-class incomes for social workers, policemen, treatment specialists, substance abuse counselors, case managers, and academics who research and write about drug addiction. Chronic alcohol and drug use can interfere with work performance and productivity and therefore represents a cost, but many people relieve their job stress with alcohol and other drugs and the consequent stress reduction may improve performance and productivity.

The illicit narcotics market is costly: people commit crimes and thus increase criminal justice costs, or get sick from drug abuse and thus increase health care costs, and so on. But that same market also provides high-paying work for some inner-city youth who are otherwise largely unemployable and therefore dependent on society for their basic needs. It has been reported that some drug dealers function as social service agents in certain impoverished inner-city areas. We know of a drug dealer in our own city, New Orleans, who uses part of his profits to feed the children in his housing project, to pay rent for women who are about to be evicted, to provide cash to help people make ends meet. He exacts a terrible price for his charity (the freedom to deal drugs in the project without interference from his neighbors) but he is considered a hero, not a villain.

Considering the costs of America's drug problem requires skepticism and sophistication in the face of bombastic declamations. In no other area of the debate over drugs does one encounter as many statistical shenanigans.

Costs to Business

"Drug abuse among American workers costs businesses anywhere from $60 billion to $100 billion a year in lost productivity, absenteeism, drug-related accidents, medical claims and theft." Thus spake ex-President George Bush in 1989, putting the White House *imprimatur* on the most commonly encountered estimate of the cost of drugs to the nation's businesses. "Variants of this statistic abound in discussions about drug abuse and are commonly repeated without qualification by the media" (Horgan, 1990: 18). So how did we come to find out that drugs cost American business $100 billion a year?

The cautious will realize that the phrase, "anywhere from $60 billion to $100 billion," implies that the true cost is known only very imprecisely. The stated uncertainty in the estimate is $40 billion, two-thirds of the lower boundary of the estimate and two-fifths of its upper boundary. It is analogous to "estimating" the weight of a person as somewhere between 120 and 200 pounds. For all the alarm about the "high costs of drugs," is this as close as we can come?

The $60 to $100 billion a year estimate derives from a single study done by the Research Triangle Institute in 1982. About 3,700 households were surveyed. Like the NHSDA surveys, the RTI survey asked respondents about their drug use in the previous week, month, year, and lifetime. The survey found that the average reported incomes of households containing at least one person who had *ever* used marijuana daily (i.e., used on 20 or more days of any 30 days *over the entire lifetime*) were 28% lower than the average incomes of similar households with no members who had ever used marijuana daily. That difference was then defined as the "income loss due to marijuana use." Extrapolated to the total population, the income loss comes out to $26 billion. Adding some additional billions to account for the estimated cost of drug related crime, health problems, and accidents, the RTI researchers then estimated the total "costs to society of drug abuse" at $47 billion (Horgan, 1990). Adjusting this number to account for inflation and population growth since 1982 brings it up to about $60 billion.

A few initial points bear emphasis. First, the RTI estimate is meant to reflect the total costs of drug abuse to society as a whole, not specifically the costs to business, as in the quotation from President Bush. Secondly, as an estimate of the total costs, it is actually much lower than at least some other estimates. Later, we consider a claim that the health care costs alone of substance abuse (including alcohol and cigarette abuse) are on the order of $240 billion. Finally, there is nothing in the RTI data to suggest that the upper end of the range of uncertainty in the estimate is $100 billion; so far as we can tell, the latter figure is derived by rounding up to the nearest plausible stopping point--an example, perhaps, of the natural tendency of bogus numbers to escalate without limit.

The RTI estimate depends heavily on the estimated income loss due to marijuana smoking and is implausible on its face. (There was no estimated "income loss" due to lifetime use of other illegal substances because a survey of 3,700 people will not contain enough users of other illegal drugs to derive a reliable estimate.) The finding suggests that, on average, persons who at any point in their lives smoked marijuana for as many as 20 out of 30 consecutive days suffer a life-long income penalty of 28% *per annum*. Since an entire third of the U.S. population has smoked marijuana at least once, this is not a reasonable conclusion. A likelier explanation is that in 1982, households who contained at least one 20-of-30-days marijuana user were, on average, considerably younger than other households, meaning that the employed adults in those households were at an earlier stage in their careers, and therefore earning less money--not because they had smoked pot regularly in the past, but because young people earn less than older, more mature workers. It is useful to recall that the baby-boomer drug culture was entering its early 30s when the RTI survey was done.

The RTI survey also included questions on current use of illegal drugs (i.e., use at least once in the month previous to the survey). One would expect the "income loss" associated with current use to be more severe than the income loss associated with use in the distant past, but there was no significant difference between the average incomes of current users of any illicit substance (including marijuana, cocaine, and heroin) and the incomes of statistically similar households containing no current users. (Recall from Chapter 2 that use of all illicit substances tends to increase modestly with education, with a small downturn among the most educated; the RTI finding is generally consistent with these NHSDA data.) The implication is that current use of illegal drugs poses no "income loss"--i.e., costs business *nothing*--whereas a marijuana binge a decade or two ago does. To emphasize, this is not a reasonable conclusion.

Inferring the costs of drug abuse from average annual incomes seems silly, but this and similar "estimation procedures" are very common in the literature. Better estimates could be derived from direct studies of the effects of drug use

28

on worker productivity, health care costs, absenteeism, and the like, yet very few direct studies of this sort have been published. This in itself is paradoxical. Every company of appreciable size has a Department of Human Resources whose function is to study such matters as productivity, absenteeism, worker well-being, etc. The general absence of firm-based studies of the effects of drug use on these variables suggests that most firms do not consider it a very serious problem.

Concerning job-related injuries, it is frequently asserted that "illegal drug users are 3.6 times more likely to be in an accident and are 5 times more likely than their drug-free counterparts to file a worker's compensation claim" (BJS, 1992: 132). The study on which these estimates are based has nothing to do with *illegal* substances; it was an informal study by the Firestone Tire and Rubber Company of employees in treatment for *alcoholism* (Morgan, 1988).

Other small, firm-based studies have come to entirely different conclusions. For example, the Utah Power and Light Company and Georgia Power Company have both reported results from studies of employees who tested positive for illegal drug use. Utah Power and Light reports that they spent an average of $215 *less* per employee per year on health benefits for drug users than for non-users (presumably because their active drug-using employees were somewhat younger). At Georgia Power, those testing positive for illegal drugs had a higher promotion rate than average; employees testing positive only for marijuana had 30% less absenteeism. More recently, the U.S. Post Office tested more than 4,000 new employees for drug use in 1987 and 1988 and has kept track of job performance since. Of the new workers tested, 9% were positive for illicit substances (which is either a surprisingly small or surprisingly large percentage). Over two years, about 15% of the positives and 11% of the negatives had been fired, a small difference. Those testing positive also took about six more sick days per year on average than those testing negative. But Horgan (1990: 22) also points out that minority postal workers tested positive at a much higher rate than non-minority workers, so the reported difference in job performance or sick days may reflect correlated effects of race as much as the effects of drug use *per se*.

In announcing its program to combat the "plague" of substance abuse, the Robert Wood Johnson Foundation claims that "the cost to business in lost productivity, absenteeism, and health insurance premiums is astronomical" (1992: 3). All estimates of the economic costs due to "lost productivity" are based on income-loss methodologies like those employed in the RTI study. The implausibility of the studies and their methods means that we do not know whether substance-users are more, less or equally productive than non-using employees. The existing evidence does not even rule out the possibility that the use of illegal substances is positive for the economy. Concerning absenteeism and direct health costs, the evidence is decidedly mixed. The conclusion that illegal drug use poses "astronomical" costs to business and society at large is a matter of faith, not of evidence. Alcohol use and abuse are almost certainly costly to business and to the nation, although even here one must be cautious. The direct costs to business of the use and abuse of illegal substances of all forms are still unknown.

Health Care Costs

"Substance abuse is responsible for $240 billion in health and disability costs each year in this country." The quotation is from the Johnson Foundation; the figure is from a study by the Center on Addiction and Substance Abuse at Columbia University and is meant to represent the total health care costs incurred annually because of substance abuse of all forms. Most of these estimated annual health care costs are due to alcohol and cigarettes; the estimated health costs of *illegal* substance use are but a fraction of the overall estimate.

If the annual health care cost of substance abuse is around $240 billion, this works out to about $1,000 per year for every man, women, and child in the country. On this basis, one can conclude either that substance abuse is an "astronomically" expensive problem or that the estimated cost is preposterous.

How does one estimate the health care costs of substance abuse? Most people would assume that these costs represent the sum total of hospital and doctor bills incurred in, plus the related expenses of, treating all the diseases and injuries that result from smoking cigarettes, drinking alcohol, or using illegal drugs. In fact, these direct treatment costs are but one of the components usually included in these estimates.

In addition to the direct treatment costs ("direct core costs"), there are many *indirect core costs* that result from the morbidity and mortality associated with substance abuse. Again, these are the costs of "income loss" resulting from days spent sick and not at work, or resulting from premature death. Thus, if a 30 year old man drops dead from a drug overdose, he has "lost" 35 years of productive life; if his expected earnings over those 35 years average, say, $30,000 per year, then the indirect cost of his premature death is 35 years x $30,000 per year, or $1,050,000, and his death from substance abuse adds a bit more than a million dollars to the estimated health care costs of substance abuse.

Most estimates of the health care costs of substance abuse also include various "other related costs," either direct or indirect. Some of these "other related costs" include the estimated cost of crimes committed by substance abusers, the property loss in motor vehicle crashes involving drug-impaired drivers, the estimated costs of incarcerating people convicted of crimes related to substance abuse, and the estimated costs of care provided by family members. Thus, many estimates include large cost components that have nothing to do with health care *per se*. Why, then, are they included? The reasoning seems to be that since substance abuse is a disease (see Chapter 8), then all costs of substance abuse are, by definition, health care costs since they derive from a health disorder.

To illustrate these cost components, imagine a cocaine-impaired driver who injures himself and two other people. The *direct core cost* is the actual outlay for the hospital treatment of the three injured people (what we would normally think of as the health care costs). The *indirect core cost* is the income loss due to days missed from work because of the injuries to the three people. *Other related costs* would include the value of the property destroyed and the cost of prosecuting and incarcerating the cocaine-impaired driver.

There are huge uncertainties in estimating each of these various cost components; the methods for estimating the health care costs of substance abuse are as indirect and inferential as the methods available for estimating productivity losses. Measuring the direct treatment costs (or "direct core costs," as above) requires that we know which health problems result from substance abuse rather than from other factors. In some cases, this is very straight-forward, for example, in cases of drug overdose, alcohol poisoning, acute drug toxicity, or Fetal Alcohol Syndrome. In other cases, the attribution is less clear. Most but not all cases of cirrhosis of the liver result from alcohol abuse; most but not all cases of lung

31

cancer result from cigarette smoking; etc. In general, substance abuse is under-diagnosed in primary care settings (McNagny and Parker, 1992; Cahill and Hodgkins, 1991; Moore and Malitz, 1986) and so a patient's records will not always make it clear that the illness results from the abuse of some substance.

In practice, all cases of various disorders (cirrhosis, lung cancer, etc.) are treated as resulting from substance abuse. The total costs of treating the diseases in these categories are then included in the overall estimate. Whether the result is a net upward or downward bias is unknown, but it increases the uncertainty.

The indirect core costs of substance abuse are even more ambiguous, since they entail estimates of the productivity or income loss due to unnecessary illness or premature death. Thus, morbidity costs are estimated as "the product of the number of persons affected, multiplied by the average income loss per person" (Rice, Kelman, and Miller, 1991: 282); mortality costs are likewise estimated as the proportion of the productive life span lost times the estimated life-time earnings. In both cases, annual mean earnings (adjusted by age and sex) for the whole population are used as the measure of income loss.

The direct treatment costs are probably the most reliably estimated. The major uncertainty here lies in deciding which costs result from substance abuse and which are due entirely to other factors. Rather surprisingly, the direct core costs are also, in general, among the smallest in the total equation. For example, one recent estimate put the health care costs of alcohol abuse at $70.3 billion dollars in 1985 (Rice, Kelman, and Miller, 1991: Table 1). The breakdown of this estimate into its components as is follows:

Direct core costs	6.8 billion
Indirect core costs	51.4 billion
Other related direct costs	9.0 billion
Other related indirect costs	3.1 billion
Total estimated costs	70.3 billion

The total estimate is dominated by the estimate of *indirect* core costs, which are the estimated income losses due to excess morbidity and premature mortality from alcohol abuse. Income losses are estimated from average annual incomes (adjusted for age and sex differences). What most people would have in mind as "health care costs of substance abuse"--the direct costs of medical treatment for substance-related disorders--amounts to less than a tenth of the total estimate.

Consider also: In estimating the costs of drugs to business, we assume that productivity is lower than average among substance abusers and use income differentials to measure the economic consequence. Yet in measuring the health care costs of excess morbidity and mortality, we assume that substance abusers are just as productive as average workers (i.e., we use average incomes to estimate the cost of "lost" days and years). The conclusion is obvious: If the productivity of substance-abusive workers is lower than average, then the estimated "indirect core costs" in these health studies are inflated, and if the productivity of substance-abusive workers is the same as the average productivity (as the health studies assume), then the estimated costs of substance abuse to business are inflated. *The basic principle seems to be that you can make any assumption you want so long as it raises the estimated costs.*

In all likelihood, the daily and lifetime productivity of persons who use enough drugs to make themselves sick is lower, and probably quite a bit lower, than the average daily or lifetime productivity of American workers at large. Using average incomes to estimate the ensuing "income loss" almost certainly overstates the costs, and probably by a rather considerable degree.

Premature mortality of substance abusers might also produce some cost *savings* over the lifetime that are worth considering. People who use enough drugs to make themselves sick might sooner or later end up in an alcohol or drug treatment program; if they die first, we save the treatment cost. The health care costs they might have later incurred are avoided; so are the costs of paying Social Security benefits once they retire. The premature deaths even of substance-abusive people are surely tragic, but in cost-benefit analysis, the economic effects of their deaths are not entirely negative. (At the very least, we should not assume that people who die prematurely from a substance abuse disorder will otherwise live out the full life expectancy.)

Using the methods described, Rice, Kelman and Miller (1991: 290) put the total cost of alcohol abuse in 1988 at $85.8 billion, and the total cost of drug abuse other than alcohol at $58.3 billion, for a total of $144 billion (cigarettes excluded). Given the points we have just made, these numbers cannot be taken seriously. The figure from the Center on Addiction and Substance Abuse adds in an estimate of the cost of cigarette smoking, corrects for inflation and population growth, and estimates the total cost of substance abuse of $240 billion a year. To stress two critical points: (1) The total figure, $240 billion per year, is dominated by the estimated costs of alcohol and tobacco abuse; abuse of illegal substances adds a fairly small proportion to the total. (2) The largest share of these estimated costs is not in direct treatment expenses but in the estimated income losses due to morbidity and mortality, which are almost certainly inflated.

The final figure, $240 billion, is given in two significant digits, implying that the true costs are known to within $10 billion in either direction. Given all the assumptions and estimations involved in the derivation of this number, the true uncertainty is obviously much larger than plus or minus $10 billion. If we set aside the estimated indirect and other related costs and focus just on the direct costs of treatment, the health care cost of alcohol and drug abuse combined (not including cigarettes) in 1988 was about $11.4 billion. This is clearly not the total cost of alcohol and drug abuse, but it is just about the only component of the cost that can be estimated more or less directly and reliably. It is also less than 5% of the total estimate.

It is also misleading to depict these costs as being entirely a "burden on the United States economy" (Rice, Kelman, and Miller, 1991: 285). All the direct core costs of alcohol, drug, and cigarette abuse represent income to the health care industry; if substance abuse now accounts for one health care dollar in four, then an end to all forms of substance abuse would create a severe recession in the health care industry. Likewise, days lost from work due to alcohol or drug use by one worker create over-time opportunities for other workers; replacing cars destroyed by drug impaired people provides employment, income, and profits to auto workers, car dealers, and the automotive industry. Even the premature death of one worker creates a promotion opportunity for some other worker.

Concerning the costs of legal substance abuse, namely alcohol and tobacco, no study of which we are aware has discounted those costs for the revenues raised in taxing alcohol and tobacco. Federal, state, and local revenues from the taxation of alcohol and tobacco exceeded $19 billion in 1990 (U.S. Bureau of the Census, 1992: 280); to this figure add another $3.4 billion in liquor license fees. It is doubtful that the total costs of alcohol and cigarette use are somehow magically reclaimed through taxation, but we do reclaim a measurable fraction. The sums raised in taxing alcohol and tobacco are of the same magnitude as the estimated direct core costs in treating substance abuse disorders.

Just as nobody really knows the total cost of substance abuse to business, nobody really knows the total cost of substance abuse to the health care system. Some of these costs can be estimated more or less reasonably; others are little more than a shot in the dark. The ones that can be estimated "more or less reasonably" add up to fairly small numbers. Most of what get counted as costs can be seen from other perspectives as benefits. None of the cost estimates subtract any possible savings nor the substantial revenues raised in taxing alcohol and tobacco. It can be concluded that health care costs are dominated by the costs of alcohol and tobacco use; in comparison, the health care costs of the abuse of illegal substances are relatively minor.

Criminal Justice Costs

Drugs and the problems they cause are now said to be overwhelming the criminal justice system. Again, the Johnson Foundation: "The criminal drug caseload has overburdened the nation's courts so severely that the civil court system...is collapsing in many states." Similar declarations can be multiplied practically without limit. Drug abuse has swamped the police, jammed the courts, and filled the prisons to overflowing.

According to estimates by the Department of Justice, the total federal, state, and local expenditure on criminal justice in 1988 was $61 billion (BJS, 1991: xiii). This is an inclusive figure for the total costs of police, courts, legal services, public defense, and corrections, and it at least sets a useful upper limit to the criminal justice costs of drug abuse, which, perforce, must be $61 billion or less.

The Department of Justice has also provided some useful estimates of the criminal justice costs of illegal drug abuse (BJS, 1992). Federal "War on Drug" expenditures specifically for law enforcement totalled $7.2 billion in 1991. (The remaining 1991 expenditure went to drug prevention and treatment programs, research and development, and other items not directly related to law enforcement.) State and local drug crime expenditures in 1988 amounted to an additional $5.2 billion (1992: 126), for a grand total of about $12.4 billion as the criminal justice costs of illegal drug abuse. (There are no doubt several additional billions resulting from alcohol use, but the Justice estimates are for illegal drug use only). Thus, the criminal justice cost of illegal drugs is roughly 20% of the total system-wide expenditure. Among the states and localities, the Department of Justice estimates that in 1988, about 10% of total criminal justice spending was for drug control (1992: 131). Those are not trivial percentages, but it would be difficult to conclude that the cost of drug-related crimes has come to swamp or dominate the overall cost of criminal justice.

Most of the criminal justice costs of drugs are not the result of drug abuse *per se* but rather the cost incurred in attempting to regulate the use of illegal substances. If the possession, sale, and use of substances such as marijuana, heroin, or cocaine were not illegal, and if in the process the price of drugs dropped so that people were not forced to commit crimes to support their drug habits, then none of these costs would be incurred (this in contrast to the health care costs, which would be incurred whether drugs were legal or not). Then too, a large share of the criminal justice expense is a fixed, not variable, cost. If there were no drug crime, existing police and other criminal justice resources could be deployed in other ways, but it is very unlikely that we would fire police officers or close prisons even if drug crime disappeared entirely.

The Costs of Alcohol and Drug Treatment

Alcohol and drug treatment is considered in Chapter 8. There are many different kinds of treatment, none particularly effective but all adding to the annual costs.

Compared to the figures that we have been discussing to this point, the annual cost of providing alcohol and drug treatment is rather small. Approximately 2 million people per year receive some form of treatment for alcohol or drug dependency (NIDA & NIAAA, 1991) at a total estimated cost in 1989 (the most recent year for which these data are available) of $1.7 billion (BJS, 1992: 133), split more or less evenly between the public and private sectors. These figures are from direct surveys of alcohol and drug treatment facilities all over the country, and while there are some problems with these surveys (some facilities, about a quarter of the total, do not respond to the survey; among those that do respond, about a third do not provide cost data), compared to the other figures with which we have been working, the estimated cost of alcohol and drug treatment is relatively solid. Thus, rounding up and making due allowance for non-reporting units in the NIDA & NIAAA survey, treating alcohol and drug disorders adds perhaps $2-$3 billion to the total annual cost.

What Do Americans Spend on Illicit Drugs?

It is often claimed that the illegal commerce in drugs is a $100 billion-a-year industry or more. "The retail value of illicit drug sales alone exceeds $100 billion [a year] and is by most accounts a growing market. Cocaine profits may have exceeded $80 billion already" (Staley, 1992: 5). Other estimates, for example by the Select Committee on Narcotics Abuse and Control, range as high as $140 billion (BJS, 1992: 36).

Are these plausible numbers? In 1991, the 100 largest U.S. corporations had total sales of $1.62 trillion, or an average of roughly $16 billion in annual sales per Top 100 corporation. The implication is that the illegal narcotics industry has become one of the nation's largest economic enterprises. Nation-wide sales of alcohol in recent years have been around $40 billion *per annum*. Does the American population spend two or three times as much on illegal drugs each year as it spends on beer, wine, and liquor? Not likely. According to the Office of National Drug Control Policy (1991), annual expenditures on illegal drugs are probably closer to $40 billion than $100 or $140 billion and *declining*.

How could one know how much Americans spend on illegal drugs? As always, any number of assumptions and guesses go into these estimates. One can use the NHSDA and other survey data to estimate the number of people who use various drugs. Corrections can be made for the under-sampling of high use groups such as prisoners. One can use similar data to estimate the frequency of use among

37

those who use at all (i.e, daily use, once a week, once a year, etc.) Multiplying the first two numbers gives an estimate of the number of "use episodes" or use "sessions." One can then make an assumption about the quantity of drugs consumed per "session" and multiply again; finally, one can make a reasoned guess about the unit prices of illegal drugs and multiply again, deriving a final number. One can also compare the resulting estimates of demand with what is known about the illicit supply, to see whether both figures come out the same.

Such is the method used by the Office of National Drug Control Policy (ONDCP) to estimate "What America's Users Spend on Illegal Drugs" (1991). According to this source, in 1990 Americans spent $18 billion on cocaine, $12 billion on heroin, $9 billion on marijuana, and $2 billion on other illegal drugs, for a total of $41 billion (1991: 3). Granted, that is a big number, although well short of the $100 billion and up figure commonly encountered. Similar estimates were made for 1988 and 1989; the report concludes that consumer spending on both cocaine and marijuana declined by 24% over the three-year period and that spending on heroin declined by 22%.

Compared to other estimates, the ONDCP report is a model of caution. The report acknowledges that "it is difficult to be precise," that "no single data source presents a comprehensive view of drug use among Americans," that "the margin of error is wide," and so on. The estimates of the number of people who use drugs and the frequency of use are derived from surveys such as NHSDA and are therefore subject to all the problems discussed in Chapter 2. Published information on the average quantity of drugs consumed per session is acknowledged to be "sparse" (1991: 9); estimates of this quantity are derived primarily from user and dealer informants and the reliability of the information is therefore unknown. Retail street prices are estimated in much the same fashion. "Researchers have rarely inquired about the amounts consumed per session or purity and cost of those drugs. The reported estimates are the best we could derive from the available data, but they should be considered to be accurate only within a broad (and unknown) band of confidence" (1991: 11).

ONDCP describes the results as "reasoned estimates based on the best available data. They stand in stark contrast to what have heretofore been informed opinions or outright guesses" (1991: 12). We hasten to agree; the report is explicit its assumptions, the quality of data, and the uncertainty of the results. One could quarrel with at least some of the report's numbers, but the caution with which the data are used instills confidence in the final product. Pending more and better data, then, we can tentatively conclude that the annual business in illegal drugs is several tens of billions. Interestingly, $40 billion a year is also about what Americans spend on alcohol ($44 billion in 1990, according to this report) or cigarettes ($37 billion in 1990), for a grand total of $121 billion on mood-altering substances of all kinds. Is it possible that the American population spends as much each year on pot, cocaine and heroin as it spends on alcoholic beverages? Such a conclusion strains credulity but it is at least a reasoned conclusion, as many other "estimates" most assuredly are not.

Summary

Estimating the cost of the "drug problem" is not easy; many complexities are involved. Oddly enough, we seem to have much better data about what Americans spend on drugs than on what their drug use costs us. The estimated cost to business depends heavily on an estimate of the "income loss" due to drug use that seems suspicious on its face; the estimated cost in health care expenses is dominated by estimates of the indirect morbidity and mortality costs that are also suspicious. Whatever the true health costs, it is clear that alcohol and tobacco abuse contribute the lion's share. If we want to justify our War on Drugs by reference to the high costs of America's drug problem, we must at the same time confess that we know very little about what these costs truly are. The believability of any given estimate is more or less inversely proportional to the shrillness with which it is proclaimed.

What qualifies as a cost from some points of view is a benefit from others; the cost of drugs to users is a benefit to dealers. And so too with nearly everything that is considered a "cost" of America's drug problem. The true costs of drugs are probably less economic than social, a possibility to which we now turn.

Four

Drugs, the Cities, and the Urban Poor

Introduction

When people speak about America's "drug problem," many have in mind its contribution to the deterioration of the inner cities and to the growth of the urban underclass. Widespread drug use has joined with crime, teen pregnancy, female headship, welfare dependency, and chronic poverty and unemployment to create a "tangle of pathology in the inner city" (Wilson, 1987: 21).

These themes are hardly new. Three decades ago, Kenneth Clark wrote of "low aspirations, poor education, family instability, illegitimacy, unemployment, crime, drug addiction, and alcoholism" as the defining characteristics of *The Dark Ghetto* (1965: 27). A steady stream of academic and media reports on urban social problems and movies such as *New Jack City* and *Boyz 'n the 'Hood* have served to reinforce the popular image of increasingly pathological inner city neighborhoods where illegal drugs are traded on every street corner and gunfire routinely punctuates the stillness of the night.

As the inner cities have become increasingly non-white, the urban drug problem has come more and more to be seen as a racial issue. Never mind that national surveys have shown very small differences in illicit drug use by race, by socio-economic status, or by city size (Chapter 2). Matters of public policy and popular alarm are rarely decided by statistical data; they are driven, rather, by images and symbolism. There is probably no image more poignant to the white majority than that of the drug-crazed young black male inflicting indiscriminate terror in a brutal, desperate attempt to satisfy his narcotic cravings.

Drug Trafficking in the Inner City

In the NHSDA data, the use of illegal drugs is more or less equally distributed across races, social classes, and geography. As suggested earlier, however, these surveys probably undercount drug users in the inner cities; also, "the problems often associated with drug trafficking and the drug economy are largely urban in character. Drug traffickers tend to recruit in densely populated urban areas. Major cities serve as principal distribution centers for a myriad of drug trafficking organizations (...) Central cities provide a variety of natural defenses against detection by law enforcement authorities" (Staley, 1992: 8). It is the concentration of the drug economy in the larger cities more than drug use that makes drugs largely an urban problem.

What makes the inner cities such fertile grounds for the emergence and growth of the drug economy? First, about three-quarters of the U.S. population now lives in metropolitan areas, so most of the demand for any consumer good will be an urban demand and drugs are no exception.

Secondly, developments in the political economy of the inner city have created a large pool of unemployed and under-employed people, mostly minority youth, for whom the drug economy provides a chance to escape poverty and enjoy a comfortable standard of living. The flow of the middle class out of the cities is now well-documented; most central city areas have been losing population since 1970. Loss of population implies a loss of jobs: "New firms are more likely to start up in outlying suburban and rural areas than in central cities" (Staley, 1992: 10). Especially troubling has been the precipitous loss of manufacturing jobs--the traditional backbone of the urban economy and the mainstay of lesser-skilled workers--and their (partial) replacement by minimum-wage jobs in the expanding service sector. Studies in the 1980s documented the increasing decline of the urban economy (e.g., Bradbury, Downs and Small, 1982; Kasarda, 1985; Bluestone and Harrison, 1986). One consequence is that joblessness among inner-city minority youth now routinely exceeds 40% or even 50%.

As an adaptation to economic decline, a large underground economy has emerged in the inner cities. Estimates of its size vary from 3% to 30% of the gross national product (Smith, 1987; Witte, 1986), but no one doubts its increasing importance in the survival of impoverished inner-city neighborhoods. Often, off-the-books work is the only work available and the only alternative to economic disaster. "The rise of the informal economy is, in essence, a reflection of the ways individuals cope with declining economic opportunities" (Staley, 1992: 21).

41

Drug trafficking is not the only work to be found in the informal economy, but it is among the larger, more lucrative components. (Some studies cited by Staley suggest that as many as a quarter of inner-city minority youth are involved in the drug trade.) The drug economy is concentrated in the cities because that is where one finds large numbers of otherwise jobless persons for whom it is the only economic game in town. The cities are also where one finds other elements of concentrated social disorganization that increase the appeal of drugs and drug trafficking (Devine and Wright, 1993; Wilson, 1987). "The rise of the drug economy in inner cities and its attendant social costs are not solely a function of a nation's wild addiction to illegal drugs, or to prohibition. Rather, the drug economy is also a function of economic developments in central cities" (Staley, 1992: 26). These trends have created a vast reserve of under-employed and under-socialized young people who are "more than willing to seize any potentially lucrative economic activity" (1992: 244), drug trafficking included.

Drug Use in the Inner City

One might also ask about the appeals of drug use to exactly this same group of people. After all, the entire point of doing drugs is to suspend ordinary awareness, to dampen, if only momentarily, the emotional oscillations of daily existence. Consider the pharmacological effects of heroin as described by John Kaplan (1983): "all your wants seem to be satisfied... great relief...you feel distant from all your problems..." Who in society has more unrelievable wants and problems than young, impoverished, uneducated, unemployed inner city people? And why, in a society that not only tolerates but actually encourages the use of "drugs" to relieve the troubles of daily life, do we find it so intolerable when poor people use drugs to relieve the miseries of poverty?

The answer lies in the apparent irrationality of so much of the behavior associated with drug use. It seems profoundly irrational when crack-addicted women exchange sex for drugs, spread AIDS, get pregnant and give birth to HIV-positive babies, or when teen-agers shoot one another to death in drug deals that have turned sour, or when large groups of apparently able-bodied men hang out drunk and stoned on the street corners while the newspapers are full of Help Wanted notices. One observer has been moved to ask, "What kind of moral universe do these people inhabit, anyway?" (Levine and Dubler, 1990: 332).

The apparently senseless behavior associated with drug use in the inner city suggests that an entire segment of the urban population has come to be indifferent to the sanctions, threats, and rewards, the laws and customs, that dictate the behavior of the rest of us. Being immune to customary threats and sanctions, the behavior of inner city drug users and dealers seems wildly out of control. Since these behaviors appear to be irrational, the fear is that nothing reasonable can be done to alter them, so repression, containment, and ultimately extinction by force loom as the only apparent alternatives. The "War on Drugs" is mainly a war against young, black, drug-using males in the central cities.

The violence of the drug trade is the most irrational feature of all. Accounts of well-armed drug gangs shooting it out on the streets without regard for bystanders have become commonplace and suggest a fundamental erosion of the value of life itself. Disgust and terror in the face of wanton brutality come easily when isolation is no longer a viable means of protection. It is one thing when urban thugs kill each other but quite another when drug-related violence threatens to overtake everyone. Pugnacious aggression against "them" is all that remains. And more and more, "they" are drug-abusive young black males who, because of the triple stigma of race, age, and addiction, are now commonly perceived to be the major threat to the well-being of the inner cities.

Drugs and the Urban Underclass

Whatever the causes, the worsening of urban conditions since 1980 has led many to look on the drug-abusive urban underclass as a growing, possibly fatal, cancer threatening the very fabric of society that must be contained and eradicated. The contempt with which drug users are viewed is evident in the favored solutions, which are to "get tough" on drugs, institute mandatory prison sentences for all drug offenses, and cut off welfare payments to recipients who test positive for drugs--as though drug users and addicts could somehow magically stop using drugs if only they possessed sufficient moral rectitude ("Just Say No").

The values and behaviors of the inner-city "drug culture" seem irrational because they have arisen as a response to grotesque social and economic conditions, not because they include drug use. If we wish to alter those values and behaviors, the only hope lies in changing the conditions that breed the responses of which

43

we disapprove. We do not need a War on Drugs nearly as badly as we need a war against the poverty, isolation and despair of inner-city life.

Many analysts (e.g., Wilson, 1987; Currie, 1985; Devine and Wright, 1993) conclude that the isolation and despair now rampant in the cities result from widespread joblessness among the inner city poor. Large-scale unemployment and the lack of viable, legitimate economic opportunities result in far more than economic deprivation; they promote a chain of events that dissolve the foundations upon which a positive and just sense of self and society are based.

Ordinary life for most people is regulated by the rules and rewards of work that pattern the days, weeks, and seasons. Cast out of that routine, people are cast out of the regulatory framework it imposes. Work and the rewards of work underpin the stability of other social institutions as well. Daily life becomes progressively deregulated as what Edelman calls the "comforting banalities" of everyday existence are destroyed. The first signs of the resulting demoralization and uncertainty are rising rates of crime, family breakdown, vagrancy, vandalism, and, of course, alcohol and drug abuse.

This "deregulation" of mainstream social mores is another way of expressing the pathology of the underclass "drug culture," a pathology best understood not as moral bankruptcy or personal deficiency but as the inevitable consequence of a structure that prevents individuals from fulfilling normal social obligations (Devine and Wright, 1993). Joblessness among inner-city non-white males now routinely exceeds 40% or even 50%; many who have a job find themselves at or near the minimum wage. Lack of meaningful jobs upon graduation undermines the rationale for staying in school; thus, drop-out rates often exceed 50%. Widespread joblessness enhances the appeal of crime or drug-dealing as an alternative; for many, the drug trade and related criminal activities now represent nearly the only route to economic success and material well-being. Ill-educated and jobless people make poor marriage partners, and so rates of illegitimacy soar. Lacking customary means by which teen-agers become adults (finish school, find work, get married), teenage girls choose to "achieve" adulthood by having babies, teenage boys "achieve" adulthood by fathering them, and jobless fathers, unable to support their offspring or their mates, leave. Joblessness creates many hours free for drinking or using drugs or committing vandalism or

44

violence. And nothing promotes "welfare dependence" quite so strongly as the lack of any viable alternative. *It is widespread joblessness, not widespread drug abuse, that has caused the deterioration of inner city life.*

Life in the context of widespread joblessness, under-employment, and extreme poverty is fundamentally *life without a future*. Lacking a future, life can quickly become a quest for the immediate gratification of present impulses, a quest for drugs. Weighing the consequences of present behavior against their future implications becomes meaningless. Arguments for staying in school, not getting pregnant, or not using drugs all require an orientation towards the future, a concern about tomorrow's consequences of today's behaviors. This is precisely the orientation that the structural conditions of the inner city have destroyed.

In this sense, the behavioral pathologies of the inner city are only symptomatic of a more general unraveling of norms and values that otherwise constrain behavior. What has arisen in the central city is a sub-culture that is essentially defined by estrangement and hostility to the norms and conventions of the larger society (Devine and Wright, 1993). To be clear, this is *not* a majority culture in the inner cities or even in their most impoverished neighborhoods. But increasingly, it is a sub-culture that defines the terms of existence for all. Drug abuse is only one small part of the process of estrangement.

Underclass youth easily discern that the successful are often those who play by a different set of rules. Why are we surprised when so many inner-city youth see no connection between hard work and material success, or when they prove indifferent to middle-class assumptions? No one can be expected to "defer" their gratifications indefinitely. The sad fact is that drug abuse is widespread in impoverished inner-city areas mainly because many of the people who live there have nothing better to do. Their lives are inherently anomic and isolated, reflecting the decline of traditional religious, educational, and family structures and values, as well as severely restricted opportunities for a better future.

"Just Say No"

The national attitude about inner-city drug users is nicely summarized in a 1992 report from the White House, *National Drug Control Strategy*:

45

"Drug use is not caused by poverty (most poor people do *not* use drugs), racism (most minority individuals do *not* use drugs), or unemployment (most people who are unemployed do *not* use drugs). Nor is it caused by being a single parent or a teenage mother, or by low educational attainment. These are circumstances that can make life harder, indeed very hard, and they are important factors in locating and influencing drug use. But to explain the drug problem by pointing to social conditions is to "victimize" drug users and deprive them of personal autonomy--the freedom and will not to use drugs. It is to deny the dignity of those who live in similar circumstances and do not use drugs. *In short, the drug problem reflects bad decisions by individuals with free wills"* (Massing, 1992: 2, emphasis added).

Likewise, most cigarette smokers die of something other than lung cancer, most abused children do not grow up to batter their own children, and most divorced women never end up in poverty. To point to predisposing social conditions is not to "deny the dignity" of those who have managed to escape their corrosive influence but to seek a reasonable, empirical understanding of why people make the choices they make. It is how one begins to understand that "Just Say No" is just not sufficient as a national drug control policy. (Whether the "Just Say No" campaign is itself responsible for the general decline in drug use documented in Chapter 2 remains an open question.)

The conclusion that the drug problem results from "bad decisions by individuals with free wills" entirely ignores the seductive appeal of drugs to poor people in the inner city. For people who lack an attainable future to which they can realistically aspire, drugs are a temporary expedient that affords escape and pleasure in an otherwise dismal life. Is this fleeting illusion of well-being not preferable to the cold realities of inner-city life? Is there really a "free will" choice to be made? Social and economic conditions in the inner cities provide powerful incentives to get drunk or high and stay that way. To ignore this point is to forego any chance at a sensible and effective drug policy.

None of this minimizes or denies the destructiveness of drugs, nor suggests that individuals do not bear responsibility for their actions. Drugs have resulted in a great deal of property and violent crime and they have had a devastating impact on some inner-city neighborhoods. However, to overlook the conditions that breed this destructive behavior and simply assert that drug addiction is a matter of "choice" dooms every intervention to failure.

Drugs, Crime, Violence, and Inner-City Youth

We have recently completed a study of guns, drugs, gangs, crime, and violence among inner-city youths in five large U.S. cities (Sheley, Wright and Smith, 1993). Two separate groups were surveyed: 835 inmates (all male) in six juvenile correctional facilities and 1,653 students (both males and females) in ten inner-city public high schools. Both samples were predominantly non-white and poor. The study provides interesting and useful details on the linkages between drug use and sales and other aspects of inner-city decay for a sample of persons normally under-represented in large household surveys.

Among the youth we studied, drug use is much more prevalent than among NHSDA youth. Alcohol and marijuana use were far more common among both the inmate and student samples than the use of harder drugs. Nearly 60% of male students had used alcohol at least a few times in the last year and a quarter had used marijuana; any use of harder drugs was reported by only 5-6%. The same patterns, albeit with much higher prevalence rates, characterized the incarcerated juveniles: 82% had used alcohol at least occasionally in the year or so before their current incarceration and 84% had used marijuana. While use of hard drugs was substantially less, it was nonetheless quite a bit higher than anything reported in NHSDA; 43% had used cocaine, 25% crack, and 21% heroin in the previous year.

Combining results across types of drugs, 10% of the incarcerated youth and 40% of the student sample had not used any drugs at all in the previous year. Complete abstinence from drugs, in other words, is characteristic of only a minority of these students and practically non-existent among the inmates. Still, the most commonly used drugs in both samples were alcohol and marijuana, not heroin or crack. And even here, 45% of the inmates and 81% of the students had not used alcohol more than a few times during the past year or two; 55% of the inmates and 93% of the students had not used marijuana more than a few times. Regular, heavy use of any of these substances was reported only by a minority of the respondents (the exception being alcohol use among the inmates).

47

As expected, the inmates were considerably more involved than students in the harder drugs. In each case, about half of those who had used the drug did so only a few times; the other half were more regular, heavier users. Also, a third of the inmates (but only 4% of the students) had been in alcohol or drug treatment programs.

Using drugs is a leisure time activity; dealing drugs is an economic pursuit undertaken for profit. For increasing numbers of inner-city youth, it appears that the drug trade has become *nearly the only well-paying economic activity available to them*. Both inmates and students were asked whether they agreed or disagreed with the statement that, "Dealing drugs is the best way for a guy like me to get ahead." Nearly two-fifths of the inmates (37%) and even one in seven (14%) of the male high school students agreed with this sentiment. A large majority of inmates (72%) and a surprisingly large percentage of male high school students (18%) had either themselves dealt drugs or worked for someone who did.

Drug use patterns themselves tell us little about the relationships among drugs, crime, guns, and violence. More extensive analysis showed that incarcerated juveniles who never even touch drugs or alcohol are nonetheless responsible for a great deal of crime and violence. For example, 44% of the inmates who had never even tried heroin had committed armed robbery; 72% of them had fired a gun at someone. Similar findings were also apparent among incarcerated non-users of cocaine, crack, marijuana and alcohol. In an era when drugs and youth crime have become inextricably linked in the popular consciousness, when the "drug problem" and the "crime problem" are seen to be nearly synonymous, it is certainly worth noting that a great deal of juvenile crime and violence are perpetrated by youth who never touch drugs or do so only occasionally.

That said, there is a definite relationship between drug use and criminal activity; users were generally more likely than non-users to have done nearly everything we asked them about. Those who had used heroin were more likely to be involved in crime, in gun ownership and use, and to believe that it is okay to shoot someone to get something one wants. Those who had used cocaine were more likely to have been involved in robbery, burglary, and property crimes committed for drug money. They exhibited greater involvement in all types of gun ownership save carrying a gun and possessing a military-style gun. They

48

were more likely to feel that shooting someone for material gain was acceptable, but they were not more likely to have fired guns during a crime or at someone. Crack users were more likely to have committed all types of crime in question but, with the exception of shotgun possession, were no more likely to be involved in gun activity or to have fired a gun during a crime or at someone.

The relation of drug use to involvement in crime and gun activities was even more pronounced for alcohol and marijuana than for the harder drugs. For all activities, users of alcohol and marijuana exceeded non-users in their level of participation. Involvement in crime and gun activity, perception of ease of gun acquisition, and assessment of the acceptability of shooting someone for material gain were progressively more likely with increased involvement in all drugs. This pattern was most pronounced for alcohol and marijuana use.

In sum, drug use is clearly associated with crime and gun activity among criminally active inner-city youth. This is the case for all five types of drug use examined individually, for heroin, cocaine, and crack use combined in index form, and for all five drugs viewed in combination. Whether this is in fact a causal relationship is more difficult to say; most studies that report an association between delinquency or crime and drug use are careful to explain "that the relationship may be spurious rather than causal" (Fagan, 1990: 184). An argument could be made that involvement in drugs leads to involvement in other crimes or leads one to possess, carry, and use firearms. At best, however, the use of drugs cannot be a necessary precondition since non-users were also heavily involved in all the activities in question.

Perhaps the most likely possibility is that drugs, guns, and criminal activity are all manifestations of the emerging inner-city underclass youth subculture, and that participation in this subculture itself is the critical variable, not participation in any particular manifestation of it. In other words, it is not that some inner-city youth get involved in drugs, which leads them causally to guns or crime, but that these youth affiliate with peer groups where hanging out, getting high, carrying guns, and committing crime have become part of the daily routine of existence. Fagan has pointed out that "the association [between drug use and crime among youth] seems to be facilitated by the strength of involvement in peer social networks where drug use and delinquency are normative" (1990: 184). No one

49

element is causally prior to any other; all result directly or indirectly from the anger, estrangement, and cultural isolation that characterize the inner cities.

Summary

People in the inner city, especially minority youth, are attracted to drug dealing and trafficking by the lack of any legitimate economic alternative; many have come to believe that the drug trade is the only way people like them can "get ahead." The same sorts of people are attracted to drug use (and thus provide a large, lucrative market for drug dealers) mainly because drugs provide some momentary escape from the harsh realities of life. For many, life in the inner cities has become life without a future. Drug use has become widespread because people with no future have nothing better to do with their time.

Many of the urban problems secondary to drug abuse, especially crime and violence, result more from the artificially high price of drugs than from drug use *per se*. Drug dealing is highly profitable mainly because drugs are relatively expensive; in turn, drugs are relatively expensive precisely because our prohibitionist, "zero tolerance" policies increase the risks associated with dealing drugs and therefore inflate the street price. If drugs were priced closer to their real market value, then fewer people would be attracted to the drug trade and fewer drug users would be forced into predatory crime in order to sustain their drug habits--these being but two possible benefits that might result from decriminalization or even legalization of most currently illegal substances. Such, in any case, is the conclusion advanced in Sam Staley's *Drug Policy and the Decline of American Cities* (1992), one of the most important treatises on the drug problem to have been published in the past decade. Granting Staley the final word on the subject of this chapter, "drug prohibition undermines the process of economic development in America's cities. The social costs of maintaining the underground drug economy through prohibition far outweigh the potential social costs of deregulation as an alternative. In effect, the unintended consequences of the drug war are so pervasive that the economic and cultural future of American cities is jeopardized" (1992: 6).

Five

Drugs and Youth

Introduction

"The rising importance of the drug problem in the eyes of the American public may well be connected to its link to children and education. In fact, public opinion polls reveal that the American public believes drug use tops the list of the 'biggest problems' public schools must deal with" (Staley, 1992: 5). The previous chapter dealt with inner-city youth; here we take up more general concerns about drugs and youth.

Drug use among the young incites special fears. "The adolescent is perhaps the most vulnerable individual confronting the growing social acceptance of drug use in the United States" (Trager, 1986: 124). We worry that young persons who experiment with drugs will progress to harder drugs and develop life-long dependencies, or that drug use will interfere with normal development, destroy motivation and self-esteem, and lead to failure in school and later life.

Drug Education and the Young

Twenty or thirty years ago, high school health and safety courses may have mentioned some of the hazards of sustained alcohol abuse but with that exception, drug education would not have been found in the high school curriculum. Today, one would be hard-pressed to find a single school in America that does not offer anti-drug education as part of its basic curriculum. Usually, anti-drug programming begins in the elementary grades and intensifies in junior high and high school. In addition to school-based programs, the Partnership for a Drug-Free America and other advocacy groups have sponsored national anti-drug media campaigns targeted mainly at youth ("This is your brain. This is your brain on drugs"). Contemporary youth are bombarded with messages about the evils of drugs and exhortations to avoid their use. If American children watch as much television as alleged, the average teen-ager is exposed to anti-drug messages several times each day.

51

So intense have our anti-drug campaigns become that there is concern among at least some observers that further efforts might prove counter-productive. "What worries a growing number of drug experts is that the cry of wolf...may backfire" (Martz, 1990: 74). One federal anti-drug bureaucrat is quoted by Martz as saying, "If the kids find out you're lying, they'll think you are lying about other things too."

Mythologies of Addiction

The specific "lie" in question is described by Martz: "In their zeal to shield young people from the plague of drugs, the media and many drug educators have hyped the very real dangers of crack [and other drugs] into a myth of instant and total addiction" (1990: 74). It is the allegedly intense addictivity of hard drugs that makes us worry about drug experimentation among the young. The image is that even casual experimentation with something like crack cocaine will often, if not invariably, lead to immediate addiction and all that addiction entails. The message is that these drugs are so good you shouldn't even try them once.

Martz reviews evidence that contradicts the "myth of instant addiction." According to the NHSDA estimates reviewed in Chapter 2, somewhere between 2.5 and 3.0 million Americans have tried crack cocaine at least once, yet the number of regular crack users (use in the previous week) is only about 850,000; the number of crack addicts is obviously even smaller. It follows that most of the people who have experimented with crack did not become even chronic users, much less addicts. "And even among current users [of crack], there are almost surely more occasional smokers than chronic abusers" (Martz, 1990: 74). Martz emphasizes an obvious point, that drug users "show a wide range of symptoms, from total impairment to almost none." By all accounts Marion Barry was a heavy user of crack if not an out-and-out addict and yet he managed to function for several years as mayor of Washington DC, the nation's 19th largest city.

The "myth of inevitable addiction" is also discussed by Kaplan in his fine if somewhat dated book, *The Hardest Drug: Heroin and Social Policy* (1983: 32-34). Kaplan quotes one "authority" to the effect that "anyone who used heroin more than six times would become an addict." We now know that such claims are exaggerated, even preposterous. "It is now clear that there exists a sizable

52

population of nonaddicted but regular heroin users who seem well integrated into society and in many ways indistinguishable from the rest of the population" (1983: 33). These regular-but-nonaddicted heroin users, called "chippers" in street argot, are probably more numerous than outright heroin addicts. Their use of heroin is recreational and self-controlled. They hold jobs, support families, pay their bills, largely "indistinguishable from the rest of the population."

The message is clear: Experimental or even extended, regular use of hard drugs such as crack and heroin does not lead to addiction in all or even most cases. This fact would be obvious to any young person growing up in a high-use neighborhood. Much of the anti-drug programming targeted at such youths is contradicted by the facts of their existence. And "if the kids find out you're lying..." As Martz concludes, "the truth [about drugs] is bad enough; there's nothing to be gained, and a lot to be lost, by hyping the dangers of drugs" past what reason and evidence can support (1990: 77).

Concerning the addictivity of various substances, nicotine is apparently the worst. Nearly 90% of casual cigarette smokers develop a nicotine addiction. Among alcohol users, about one in eight is a problem drinker. Crack, cocaine, and heroin are more addictive than alcohol but less addictive than nicotine; among casual users of these harder drugs, the number who will eventually become addicted is estimated to be somewhere between one in six and one in three.

The NHSDA surveys show higher rates of drug use among late teens and early adults than among any other age group. Drug use is low among early teens, climbs steadily among late teens and early adults, and then drops off rather sharply after age 25. Drug experimentation is relatively common among the young; hardly anybody uses drugs for the first time after age 25. The sharp drop-off in use after age 25 also shows that drug use is something most youth grow out of. Thus, much that we seek to achieve through in-school and media campaigns seems to happen anyway in the natural course of affairs.

Youth, Drugs, and "Pushers"

Part of the concern about youth and drugs is the presumed susceptibility of young people to "pushers." But the "pusher" is also a myth (Kaplan, 1983: 25-32).

53

The myth is that young people get hooked on drugs because pushers encourage experimentation with free starter samples to promote addiction and ensure steady customers, just as cigarette companies once routinely gave away free cigarettes.

That is not the way drug use begins or addiction actually happens. Most drug dealers say they strongly prefer to deal exclusively with their established customers, thereby incurring much lower legal risks. Most dealers understand that standing around outside schools passing out free "starter samples" would be foolhardy. Also, a "pusher" would have to give away very large quantities in order to get someone addicted; people normally do not get hooked with one or two casual administrations. Finally, user demand is sufficiently high that it does not need to be stimulated; it is a rare drug dealer with sufficient unsold (or unsellable) drugs to just give them away in the hopes of creating new customers.

Drug use spreads via peer influence where usage is already widespread, not from the activities of pushers or dealers. Interviews confirm that the most common initial exposure is via "best friends," with siblings a second common source. (This is true of both poor and middle class youth, and true for alcohol and marijuana as well as harder drugs.) Youth experiment with drugs mainly because other youth, not pushers and dealers, have convinced them that it is "cool."

Again, Kaplan: "Probably the most common scenario of an addict's first heroin use is that he was walking or driving around with nothing much to do when he either ran into or visited a friend who, he discovered, was preparing to 'shoot up.' He was invited to join...and, without thinking much about the matter, he accepted. Why he [accepted] is a complex question, since there are many who refuse such offers. Perhaps he was bored or curious, but one common reason was that he came from an area where heroin was regarded as a nervy, 'stand-up' thing to do" (1983: 28). This scenario for the onset of drug use is every bit as telling today as it was a decade ago. Drug use spreads among the young through peer pressure and peer influence more than any other factor.

Anti-Drug Programming: CAN-DO

Many of the dynamics of drug use, drug experimentation, and peer influence are revealed in a study of an anti-drug program targeted at disadvantaged youth in

Cincinnati (Wright, 1991). The Community and Neighborhood Drug Offensive (CAN-DO) was a national demonstration project sited in nine large U.S. cities designed to promote the use of local volunteers to bring "zero-tolerance" anti-drug programming to high risk central city neighborhoods. In Cincinnati, over 200 volunteers were enlisted in the effort, with program activities largely focussed in the Over-the-Rhine section of the city.

Over-the-Rhine had suffered significant recent deterioration and was the poorest and most troubled neighborhood in the city when CAN-DO began. In the 1980 census, the poverty rate in Over-the-Rhine stood at 62.3%, making it one of the poorest neighborhoods in any U.S. city. CAN-DO anti-drug activities were concentrated in one particular junior high school (sixth, seventh and eighth grades) in the neighborhood, which we shall call St. Vincent's (a pseudonym).

CAN-DO's anti-drug programming at St. Vincent's was intense. Each week, volunteers and staff provided drug education classes; participation was mandatory. The curriculum focussed on the hazards of drug use, the health effects of drugs, alternatives to drugs, why people use drugs, "just say no," and the general social havoc resulting from widespread drug use. Drug-free zones were created around the school and elsewhere in the neighborhood and special anti-drug activities were undertaken monthly.

Students were also closely involved in designing a media campaign targeted at other youth in the neighborhood. This project consumed an entire semester (January to June). A local advertising agency worked directly with students to develop a campaign slogan, approach, posters and billboards that would bring the CAN-DO zero-tolerance drug message to the larger community. This involved focus groups, art projects, and related activities involving students and staff from both CAN-DO and the advertising agency.

By late spring, 1991, the outlines had gelled. The centerpiece would be outdoor billboards in the target area, supplemented by coverage on local radio stations. In May, a final list of possible themes and slogans had been decided, all having emerged from projects done by the students. The media campaign was unveiled across the street from the school in June, 1991. The campaign slogan, "Just Chill--Drugs Kill," had been created by one of the students, as had the subsidiary slogan, "Just DON'T Do It!" (this an intentional take-off on the Nike sports shoe commercial). The billboard featured a street scene with about a dozen students, all of whom became instant celebrities among their peers. The sense of pride and achievement that the project had instilled was unmistakable.

The unveiling was covered by a local rap radio station and was also featured on the evening television news. Press coverage was extremely favorable. Students gave a press conference; several were interviewed by a local news anchorman. All of them were also introduced to a popular rap DJ. The entire point was to show that young people could be strongly anti-drug and still be very "cool."

As anti-drug programming efforts go, the project was commendable. It was community-based and intensive; it offered alternative, positive role-modelling; it involved young people in a highly visible community-wide anti-drug effort. If ever a program would help young people "just say no," this was it.

The ending of this story is as dismal as the beginning was hopeful. Before-after survey data showed that alcohol, marijuana, and tobacco use *increased* during the summer following the campaign. The trend was *stronger* among students who had participated than among those who had not, and among the specific students featured on the "Just Chill-Drugs Kill" billboard, the trend was stronger still.

Why? Analysis revealed some of the reasons why anti-drug programming of the CAN-DO sort is not generally effective. First, most students said they knew where they could buy alcohol if they wanted to; large minorities also knew where they could buy marijuana and hard drugs. In short, drugs were readily available. The substantial majority reported that at least some of their friends used alcohol; a quarter had friends who used marijuana; a tenth had friends who used hard drugs. Half had been to a party in the last year where alcohol was served; a third had been to a party where marijuana was being used. About one in six had been involved in drug dealing at some time.

CAN-DO style programming competes poorly against the incentives young people have to begin using drugs. In Over-the-Rhine, one is struck by the number of liquor stores and advertisements. Alcohol and cigarettes are readily available, socially sanctioned, and legal (at least for adults). Illicit drugs such

56

as marijuana and crack are nearly as available as alcohol and tobacco. Parental drug use provides a model for behavior; peer pressure is always consequential and sometimes overwhelming. Finally, alcohol and drug use gives pleasure. Drugs fill the summer hours; alternatives are in short supply in inner-city neighborhoods everywhere. In the face of these structural and behavioral factors, anti-drug classes and media campaigns cannot be very effective in preventing the onset of drug experimentation and use among the young.

Youth who experiment with crack or heroin or marijuana or even alcohol are taking certain undeniable risks in order to enjoy certain undeniable pleasures (euphoria, acceptance by peers, etc.) Anti-drug programming can make young people more aware of the risks but not reduce the pleasures. In turn, taking risks to achieve pleasure is not unusual behavior; many high-risk activities (sky-diving, bungi-jumping, drag racing, skiing, even swimming) are undertaken to provide pleasure or to give relief from the boredom of everyday life. Judged in this light, experimentation with drugs is not much different from many of the other things young people do in the process of exploring and defining themselves. And like many of those other things, drug use is something most youth grow out of.

It is even possible that anti-drug programming increases the curiosity of young people about drugs. Nothing increases a child's interest in something more than being told it is something they shouldn't do. Part of the appeal is *precisely* that drugs are illegal. Most college students we have informally surveyed report that they consume less alcohol as college students than they did as high school students; once the behavior is legal and socially acceptable, it is no longer as much fun. The concern is that anti-drug programming can increase the mystique of drug use. After all, everything adults define as naughty or dangerous is fun by definition; if it were not fun, there would be no point in warning youth away from it. A more casual attitude about such matters might reduce, rather than enhance, the appeal of drugs to the young.

Summary: The Prevalence of Drug Use Among the Young

Hysteria about drug use among young people can make us forget that most young people never even experiment with drugs, much less become regular users or addicts. A recent survey of persons in the prime drug-using years (ages 19-28) showed that only a bit more than a quarter had used any illegal substance any time in the previous year, nearly all of which was marijuana (Martz, 1990). Even among the highest use ages, the proportions using harder drugs such as cocaine, LSD, or heroin are never more than a few percentage points. Most young people will try alcohol at least once before they are legally eligible to drink, but with that exception, even casual experimentation with drugs is something the majority never do; only three or four young people in a hundred ever get around to experimenting with drugs more serious than marijuana.

The preferred drug among youth is alcohol and has been for as long as we have gathered data. Alcohol use among the young is a serious social problem. A fairly large minority of the young will also experiment with marijuana. The proportion of young people who have used marijuana in the last year (about a quarter) is in the same range as the proportion of the adult population who have used marijuana (about a third). There are some young people, a few percent at most, who will also experiment with hard drugs, and an even smaller number who will become regular users or even addicts. The usual pattern of drug use is relatively high rates of use in the early adult years and fairly sharp declines as people mature into adulthood.

We think it would be reprehensible not to instruct youth in the hazards of drug use. Given the use patterns, alcohol and tobacco should dominate this effort. But "there's nothing to be gained and a lot to be lost" through alarmist hyperbole. Dispassionate presentation of the facts would normally be sufficient to impart the necessary message but at the same time not further stimulate the natural curiosity of young people about drugs and their effects.

Six

Drugs, Crime, and Criminal Justice

Introduction

Drug-related violence and widespread property crime have served as fundamental motivating tenets in America's century-long war against drugs (Inciardi, 1986; Musto, 1987; Nurco, Kinlock, and Hanlon, 1990). Usually, drug-induced crime is associated with ethnic minorities whose allegedly deviant values threaten to undermine the fabric of society (Inciardi, 1986). In the late 19th century it was the Chinese and opium. By the turn of the century, "Negroes" had become the target (Primm, 1992). During Prohibition it was ethnic immigrants. Later, communist influence was thought to lurk behind the escalating use of heroin, marijuana, and hallucinogens (Musto, 1987). Now it is young African-American males and South American drug lords who are singled out for blame.

The linkage between drugs and crime is by no means fictional nor is popular concern simply reducible to racism and scapegoating. Likewise, crack continues to take a very real toll. Nonetheless, rhetoric often substitutes for evidence and critical reflection. The assertion that "drugs cause crime" proves misleading; the connection is more complicated and subtle than that.

Establishing the Drug-Crime Connection

That there is an association between drug use and crime is easily demonstrated. Consider the following points, all well-established and well-known:

● In a third of all violent crime victimizations reported in 1991, victims reportedly "thought" their assailants were under the influence of drugs or alcohol at the time the crime was committed (BJS, 1992).

● The above figure is consistent with a 1989 BJS survey (1993: 4) showing that a fourth of convicted jail inmates, a third of state prisoners, and two-fifths of incarcerated youths in long-term correctional facilities were under the influence of an illegal substance at the time they committed the offense for which they were incarcerated. When one adds alcohol, the figures increase substantially.

● Data from the National Institute of Justice's Drug Use Forecasting (DUF) survey, a multi-city arrestee drug screening program, further support these findings. In the 1991 DUF sample of male arrestees from 24 U.S. cities, positive drug tests for illicit substances ranged from 36% (in Omaha) to 75% (in San Diego). Among women, for whom only 21 cities reported data, the range was 45% (in San Antonio) to 79% (in Cleveland).

● Driving under the influence of intoxicating substances (DUI), most often alcohol, represents the single most frequent criminal charge in the United States. In 1986, DUI charges were responsible for approximately 1.8 million arrests and, according to the National Highway Traffic Safety Administration, alcohol and other drugs were implicated in 40% of the 46,056 motor vehicle fatalities that occurred during that year (BJS, 1988).

● Studies of drug use and criminal involvement in Baltimore and California (BJS, 1992: 4) provide further confirmation. These studies focussed on criminal behavior among heroin addicts during periods of use and abstinence. During abstinent periods, criminal activity was relatively low. During active use periods, criminal involvement showed a four-to-six-fold increase. Similar studies done in Miami and New York found the same basic patterns (Inciardi, 1986: 122-132; Faupel and Klockars, 1987; Johnson *et al.*, 1985).

● Inmate surveys document high rates of current and long-term alcohol and drug use among offender populations. With respect to lifetime use, BJS survey data indicate that 78% of jail inmates, 80% of state prisoners, and 83% of youth offenders in long-term juvenile justice facilities have used drugs (BJS, 1993: 7).

● While only 10% of non-drug-using inmates reported having had illegal sources of income in the year preceding their incarceration, almost half of the inmates reporting daily major drug use indicated illegal sources of income (Akers, 1992).

● Most clients in both the Drug Abuse Reporting Program (DARP) and the Treatment Outcome Prospective Study (TOPS), two large-scale multi-site national studies of drug treatment conducted during the 1980s (see Gerstein and Harwood, 1990), reported having been arrested or incarcerated or having engaged in crime for economic gain prior to entering treatment (BJS, 1992: 4).

● Alcohol and drug use is an important factor in victimization. Studies have found that in 76% of manslaughters and 50% of sexual assaults, offenders, victims, or both had been using alcohol or drugs before the incident (BJS, 1993).

● Among violent offenders in state prisons, 26% of those who were using drugs reportedly victimized someone on drugs, 40% who had been drinking victimized someone who also had been drinking, and 17% of offenders who were both drinking and using victimized someone drinking and using (BJS, 1993: 6).

Thus, there is an incontrovertible relationship between drugs and crime. Users report greater involvement in crime and are more likely to have criminal records. Persons with criminal records are more likely to report being drug users. Crimes rise in number as drug use increases, and high levels of criminal activity are strongly related to the frequent use of drugs and the use of multiple drugs.

Disentangling the Drug-Crime Connection

The relationship between drugs and crime may be quite direct and causal (e.g., when junkies steal to support their habit). In other cases, the relationship may be indirect or even spurious, drug use and criminal activity both being aspects of some larger deviant lifestyle. Or drug use may be wholly independent of criminal activity, as in the case of casual or recreational drug users who never engage in any form of predatory criminal activity. Finally, the purchase, possession, or use of any illegal substance is by definition a crime. The latter, sometimes called "technical offenses," constitute crimes solely because of our policies concerning drug prohibition and regulation.

Even setting aside technical drug offenses, there are at least four analytically distinct ways in which drugs and crime might be connected:

(1) The pharmacological effects of certain drugs may induce individuals to commit crimes;

(2) Crimes may be committed to support one's drug habit;

(3) Some crimes may be committed in connection with the traffic in drugs; and

(4) Drugs and drug abuse can be otherwise implicated in criminal behavior, though not responsible for or causally related to it.

Technical Drug Offenses

Many of these connections exist because of drug policies, not because of the pharmacology or behavioral correlates of drug use. One important link is definitional; the manufacture, cultivation, distribution, and possession of illicit drugs such as marijuana, heroin, and cocaine are crimes because drug policy defines them as criminal violations. Decriminalization of drugs would wipe out the larger part of this entire category of criminal behavior, one that now swallows a substantial share of the nation's law enforcement resources.

The nation's drug laws are a complex patchwork of federal, state and local statutes. While specifics vary, laws pertaining to illicit and controlled substances fall into three general categories: (1) possession or use, (2) production prohibitions, and (3) distribution offenses.

There are hundreds of other federal and state laws that govern activities that relate to (but are separate from) drug possession, use, and trafficking. These include laws that regulate use or possession of otherwise legal chemicals used in the manufacture of illicit drugs; drug paraphernalia laws covering possession and sale of objects such as pipes, rolling papers, roach clips, etc.; laws pertaining to money laundering, corruption, and racketeering that result from the drug trade; otherwise legal drug diversion laws; and laws pertaining to driving under the influence (DUI) of legal and illegal substances.

Enforcement occurs through the combined efforts of federal, state, and local jurisdictions and agencies. In 1990, 12,000 local law enforcement agencies joined state and federal agencies like the Drug Enforcement Administration (DEA), Customs Service, Coast Guard, and U.S. Postal Service to enforce the nation's drug laws (BJS, 1993: 11).

Most drug arrests are made by local and state authorities. In recent years, local and state authorities have made over a million arrests for drug law violations *per annum*, a 50% increase since the early 1980s (BJS, 1993: 9). In a typical year, about two-thirds of these arrests are for mere possession.

As arrests increase, so does the proportion of inmates doing time on drug charges. In 1983, 9% of the jail population was incarcerated on drug charges; by 1989, the figure had more than doubled to 23%. Among state prisoners, the increase was even larger, from 6% to 22% (BJS, 1993: 18). Much of the increase reflects from mandatory sentencing. The impact on the courts has been substantial. In New York City, the percentage of felony indictments stemming from drug law violations increased from 25% to 40% between 1985 and 1987, while in Washington, drug law violations went from 13% to 52% of all felony indictments between 1981 and 1986 (Nadelmann, 1989).

At the national level, enforcement of drug laws is primarily the responsibility of the Drug Enforcement Agency (DEA). Between 1979 and 1990, DEA arrests doubled from about 10,000 to more than 21,000 (BJS, 1992: 158). In 1991, the DEA seized 387 drug manufacturing or processing laboratories, eradicated 139 million marijuana plants, confiscated 150,000 pounds of cocaine, 236,000 pounds of marijuana, over 2,400 pounds of heroin, and more than 30 million dose units of stimulants and hallucinogens, and seized $53 million in drug-related assets.

Jurisdiction for federal drug enforcement efforts is not restricted to the DEA. Other agencies make arrests for drug violations, detain aliens found to possess drugs, confiscate illicit substances, and engage in crop eradications and seizures. All told, between 1980 and 1990, the number of persons convicted for violations of federal drug laws increased from about 5,000 to more than 16,000, a 218% increase that accounts for over three-fifths of the total growth in federal convictions during the decade. As a result, drug law violators comprised only 22% of federal prison admittees in 1980 but 58% in 1990.

Other Drug-Related Offenses

In addition to technical offenses, drugs are implicated in a variety of other violent, predatory, property, and even so-called victimless crimes. In some cases, drugs are assumed to act as a critical pharmacological inducement to commit crime. The evidence in favor of this proposition is somewhat limited; it consists mainly of horror stories about the violence-inducing properties of heroin, cocaine and, more recently, PCP ("angel dust"). Many clinicians and drug treatment experts dispute such claims and feel that the case is overstated (see, e.g., Nadelmann, 1989: 941).

The evidence on the violence-engendering properties of alcohol use is more persuasive. A number of studies have explored the connection between alcohol and familial and other forms of violence (see Nadelmann, 1989: 941). These studies document a statistical association but not a causal one (see BJS, 1992: 5). Violence is more common among families where the adults drink alcohol, but this does not establish that the higher rate of violence results directly from alcohol use (as opposed to other correlated factors).

A second connection involves people who commit crimes to support their drug habits. Property crimes figure prominently here, but violent crimes and victimless crimes such as prostitution may be similarly motivated. In recent years, local jurisdictions have reported a growing proportion of arrests for prostitution; further analysis reveals that female drug users have increasingly resorted to prostitution to raise money or barter for drugs, especially crack.

While informal police estimates often suggest that as much as 50% to 80% of all property crime is committed to raise money for drugs, there is little solid empirical evidence to support such claims. A 1989 survey of convicted jail inmates indicated that only 13% had committed their current offense to raise money for drugs (BJS, 1992). Likewise, a study of incarcerated juvenile offenders showed that more than half had *never* committed a crime specifically to get drug money; only about 10% said that they had done so regularly (Sheley, Wright, and Smith, 1993). Earlier data from incarcerated adult felons showed a similar pattern (Wright and Rossi, 1986). On the other hand, there is a four-to-six fold increase in criminal activity among heroin addicts during active use periods. So while at least *some* property crime is drug-motivated, no one knows for sure just how much. Most property crimes are never solved by the police, and so the imputation of a specific reason why they were committed is gratuitous.

64

Many of the crimes committed to obtain drug money are also stimulated by our current prohibitionist policies, which increase the risk of drug trafficking and therefore raises prices (see, e.g., Staley, 1992; Nadelmann, 1989). Some users may reduce or eliminate their drug consumption in the face of higher prices, but others continue to use at the same rate and cover the difference by engaging in additional predatory activity. We do not know very much about the elasticity of the demand for drugs with respect to their price, but it is fairly obvious that prohibition raises the price and that higher prices can lead to more crime.

Yet another connection is crimes committed in association with the distribution or sale of drugs. This connection has been linked to escalating homicide rates. Recent studies in New York, Washington, Miami, Detroit, Atlanta, Philadelphia and other cities indicate that alcohol and drugs are implicated in between a quarter and half or more of homicides, with many being directly related to drug trafficking and drug-gang activity (BJS, 1992: Ch. 1). As a recent BJS report summarizes, "violence is used to protect or expand markets, intimidate competitors, and retaliate against sellers or buyers who are suspected of cheating. To avoid being arrested and punished for trafficking, drug dealers commit violent crimes against police and threaten informants and witnesses" (1992: 5).

The problem here is that under current policy, the drug market is inherently undisciplined, thus controlled by force and intimidation. This might be compared with alcohol: When alcohol was prohibited, the market was also a violent free-for-all; once legalized, the market became highly disciplined and readily controlled by conventional law enforcement, regulation of businesses with licenses to sell and dispense alcohol, and taxation. Decriminalization would take much of the profit out of the drug trade, and while some marketers would likely turn to other illegal and violent criminal activities, many perhaps would not.

Drugs are also implicated in criminal behavior when both drugs and crime are components of a wider constellation of deviant activities. There is substantial literature to indicate that involvement in crime often *precedes* drug use and that "the relationship between drugs and crime is developmental rather than causal" (BJS, 1992: 4; see also Akers, 1992; Huizinga, Menard, and Elliott, 1989; Johnston, O'Malley, and Eveland, 1978; Sheley, Wright, and Smith, 1993). A recent BJS study (1993: 7) found that 60% of the state prisoners who had ever

65

used a major drug (heroin, methadone, cocaine, PCP, or LSD), had not done so until *after* their first arrest, and that half of the regular hard drug users did not commence their drug use until a year or more following their first arrest. Once drug abuse becomes established in the behavioral repertoire, however, it appears to have a "multiplier" effect on continued criminal activity (Akers, 1992; Anglin and Hser, 1987; Anglin and Speckart, 1988).

Summary

Drugs are clearly factors in numerous crimes; there is a strong correlation between drug use and criminal involvement. Nonetheless, establishing causality is difficult. For many persons, criminal activity is a direct outgrowth of their drug use. For others, criminal activity predates drug use or remains largely independent of it. For still others, drug activity constitutes the preferred mode of profitable criminal enterprise and has very little to do with drug use *per se*.

A large (but essentially unknown) proportion of drug-related crime and all technical drug offenses result directly from our failed effort to prohibit sale, possession, and use of illegal drugs. Decriminalization and controlled distribution, coupled with an increased emphasis on treatment, would almost certainly attenuate the drug-crime connection. At the same time, alcohol is implicated in a great deal of crime despite being legal, and so it would be foolish to assume that decriminalization would wipe out the connection completely.

Drugs become a social problem mainly when drug users find they must resort to crime or commit violence in order to sustain their drug use habits. Even today there would be rather little concern about the "drug problem" were it not for the crime and violence perpetrated against middle class people that drugs seem to have occasioned. If the "drug problem" and its consequences could be confined to the central city ghettos, it is not clear that anybody would really care.

It is not correct to argue that drug addiction is itself responsible for the American crime rate. Still, drug addiction is responsible for a lot of crime. In the Wright-Rossi (1986) study of adult felons, more than three-quarters were alcoholics, drug abusers, or both. Numerous other studies have confirmed this basic fact. A fair summary is that most drug users commit relatively little or no crime

66

(excepting their technical violations of drug laws), but a small proportion of hard drug abusers commit a tremendous amount of crime (Nurco *et al.*, 1990). It is mainly the resulting fear, not the spread of drug use *per se* or its effects on impoverished communities, that has given us our War on Drugs.

Recent research on incarcerated youth and on male high school students (Sheley, Wright, and Smith, 1993) shows strong but complicated linkages between drug use, drug dealing, and criminal or violent activity; numerous other studies show similar effects (see, for instance, Akers, 1992; Inciardi, 1986; Nurco *et al.*, 1990). Use of alcohol and illicit drugs was relatively common in both the felon and high school samples, but very few in either sample could be described as hard-core, regular drug users. Among juvenile inmates, criminal activity increased with level of drug use; still, even non-users were fairly active criminals. The large majority of the inmates (72%) and a notable minority of male high school students (18%) had either themselves dealt drugs or worked for someone who did. Firearms are a common element; 68% of the inmates agreed that people who deal drugs are *always* armed. Eighty-nine percent of the inmate dealers and 75% of the student dealers had carried guns and firearms are a frequent medium of exchange in the drug trade at all levels.

Drugs worsen the problems of the inner city but are symptoms (not causes) of more general social woes (Chapter 4). Drug use has become a part of the inner-city culture but not its defining or distinguishing feature. To hold the "drug epidemic" directly responsible for America's crime problem is to search for scapegoats, not solutions.

Seven

_____

Drugs and Health

Introduction

America's drug problem inheres largely in the effects of chronic drug use on health and well-being. Any substance in common use will be abused by some people and can lead to health problems. Prescription drugs such as Valium, psychotropics, barbiturates, anabolic steroids, etc. are commonly abused with serious health consequences; likewise, many over-the-counter cough syrups, nasal sprays, laxatives, sleeping aids, and so on are widely abused. A comprehensive account of health problems secondary to the abuse of both legal and illegal substances is beyond the scope of this chapter; our focus is on the most common health problems known to be associated with the most commonly abused drugs.

Drugs cause health problems in two entirely separable ways. The first is the direct effect of various drugs on the body's organ systems. The body contains trillions of cells, highly differentiated by function and therefore by the chemistry that defines them; the chemistry of the various cells is affected in different ways by different drugs. When drugs disrupt cell chemistry and therefore function, and when the resulting dysfunction causes distress or disease, then we are correct to refer to that distress or disease as the direct effect of drug use.

A second and increasingly important way that drugs cause health problems is when the behavioral correlates of drug use cause disease. Intravenous injection of heroin or cocaine (or both: the mixture is called a "speedball") does not in itself cause hepatitis or AIDS; these infections result from using infected needles. In these cases, disease does not result from the direct action of abused substances on cell chemistry but from behaviors that are associated with drug use.

The Direct Health Effects of Drug Use

Just as the costs of substance abuse are dominated by tobacco and alcohol abuse, and not by the abuse of illegal substances, so too are the health effects of tobacco

68

and alcohol abuse far more consequential than those resulting from the abuse of all illegal substances combined. Indeed, in comparison to the health effects of alcohol and cigarettes, the toll taken by all illicit substances combined is minor.

Alcohol: Moderate use of alcohol promotes health and longevity; immoderate use is associated with a wide variety of circulatory, endocrinological, hepatic, neurological, and other system failures. Alcohol is metabolized in the liver and changed to fat; thus, even in small quantities, alcohol consumption results in deposits of fat in the cells of the liver, a condition known as "fatty liver." If consumption is halted, these deposits disappear; over a sustained period of alcohol use, however, the fat deposits will begin to interfere with normal hepatic (liver) function. The rotund bellies of heavy drinkers often bespeak advanced stages of liver disease. A sufficiently long and chronic pattern of alcohol consumption will result in the death of liver cells (necrosis) and ultimately cirrhosis, liver failure and death. Most cases of cirrhosis of the liver result from alcohol abuse; in fact, the rate of liver cirrhosis (in various cities, counties, states, or even countries) is a reliable indicator of relative rates of alcohol abuse.

Heavy use of alcohol is also associated with hypertension (high blood pressure) and other heart and circulatory disorders, with various gastrointestinal disorders such as ulcers, colitis, and gastritis, and with endocrinological failures, especially of the pancreas (which leads to diabetes). There is also evidence that alcohol and its contaminants are carcinogenic. Alcohol abuse is also harmful to the central nervous system, with effects ranging from tremors to seizure disorders that mimic epilepsy to degenerative disorders of the brain. Pure alcohol is highly toxic; a sufficient quantity of alcohol in any form will produce acute alcoholic toxicity and frequently death from respiratory failure (acute alcoholic toxicity is, in essence, an overdose). Finally, use of alcohol by pregnant women can result in Fetal Alcohol Syndrome. (Research on FAS continues; at present, a "safe" level of consumption for pregnant women has not been ascertained and the prudent course of action is to avoid all alcohol during pregnancy.)

A wide range of psychiatric disorders are also caused or exacerbated by sustained use of alcohol and other drugs; rebound depression, psychotic episodes, and depression secondary to withdrawal are the classic examples. A number of psychiatric illnesses are strongly associated with chronic alcohol abuse, including

69

delusions, alcohol-induced psychosis, organic brain syndrome, and Korsakoff's disease (alcoholic dementia).

There is a second tier of alcohol-related health problems that result from behaviors associated with alcohol use. For example, heavy drinkers are often physically inactive and eat poorly. Many central nervous system pathologies associated with alcohol are actually the result of vitamin deficiencies. Heavy drinkers tend also to be heavy smokers; in research on health effects of alcohol, it is sometimes hard to separate the effects of alcohol *per se* from the effects of all the other harmful things alcoholics do to their bodies.

Cigarettes: The health problems associated with smoking are well-known; public concerns over the deleterious health effects of tobacco smoke date at least to 1604 (Jarvik and Schneider, 1992: 337). Cigarette smoke is a major lung irritant and over 200 carcinogenic (cancer-causing) chemicals have been identified in tobacco smoke. Smoking causes lung diseases ranging from chronic bronchitis to emphysema to lung cancer. There is also evidence linking tobacco consumption to cancers of the pharynx, mouth, esophagus, stomach, intestine, pancreas and bladder. In addition, smoking is implicated in various cardiovascular disorders ranging from coronary heart disease to peripheral vascular disorders. Smoking by pregnant women retards fetal growth and results in low birth weight babies. Smokeless tobacco is less damaging to the lungs but causes cancers of the mouth and probably gastrointestinal ailments also.

Cigarettes are the number one preventable cause of premature death in the United States. In 1990, 2.1 million Americans died; about 400,000 of those deaths were the result of cigarette and tobacco use. Alcohol abuse accounted for about 100,000 deaths, and abuse of all other drugs accounted for only 20,000 deaths. In the same year 35,000 people died from the homicidal, suicidal, or accidental abuse of firearms, fewer than a tenth the number taken to the grave by cigarettes.

Marijuana: Like tobacco, marijuana is usually smoked and so many of the direct health effects of marijuana are similar to those of tobacco. Marijuana smoke is probably even more irritating to the lungs than tobacco smoke and has higher levels of tar and various carcinogens, but very few people smoke the equivalent of two packs of marijuana cigarettes a day. Sustained heavy use of marijuana

70

has also been linked to sexual dysfunction, various disorders of the reproductive system, and possible cognitive impairment, although most of the evidence comes from studies in laboratory animals. On the other hand, "there is a substantial body of evidence that moderate use of marijuana does not produce physical or mental deterioration" (Grinspoon and Bakalar, 1992: 239); sustaining evidence dates as far back as the 1890s. Some marijuana users are known to suffer short-term anxiety attacks while under the influence of the drug, and first-time marijuana users sometimes (although rarely) suffer a rather mild and transient depression, but with these very rare and minor exceptions, "dangerous physical reactions to marijuana are almost unknown. No human being is known to have died of an overdose [of marijuana]" (Grinspoon and Bakalar, 1992: 241).

Cocaine and Heroin: The health effects of substances such as cocaine and heroin are known less certainly than those of alcohol and tobacco because most abusers of these drugs also drink large amounts of alcohol and smoke heavily, making it difficult to separate the effects. (Thus, we do not have a very clear picture of the effects of cocaine on fetal development because it is practically impossible to find pregnant women who use cocaine but do not also drink heavily.)

Cocaine use has been linked to cerebrovascular disease and to ischemic (heart) disorders, among them heart arrhythmias, coronary artery disease, and congestive heart failure, although the associations are not strong and the mechanisms are poorly understood. Metabolites of cocaine have also been associated with colitis, liver disease, and renal (kidney) dysfunction. Chronic cocaine use over an extended period may also be associated with central nervous system dysfunction and acute paranoid psychosis. Heroin is apparently not toxic to body tissues, but there is some evidence that heroin use can cause endocrinological and neurological damage. Skin ulcers and infections, often serious, can develop from injecting heroin (or any other drug) with unsterile syringes, as can hepatitis.

Like chronic alcoholics, chronic cocaine and heroin abusers are frequently malnourished and debilitated, increasing their risk of nutritional and vitamin deficiency disorders and infections.

Et Cetera: There is practically no substance in common use that is not also abused to the detriment of physical well-being. Inhalable substances such as glue, aerosols, paint thinners, solvents and gasoline are commonly used by many people to get high. The practice has been linked to health problems such as arrhythmia, liver and kidney failure, lung damage, myopathy, neuropathy and anemia (Shuckit, 1989). Another inhalable substance is methamphetamine hydrochloride ("ice"). So far, the direct health effects of "ice" have only been investigated in laboratory animals but they are not likely to be positive in humans. Recent publicity surrounding the death of Lyle Alzado (a football star) has called attention to the deleterious health effects of anabolic steroids. Steroid use has been linked to a variety of psychiatric illnesses; the somatic effects range from trivial (premature baldness, acne) to the profound (disorders of the reproductive system, hepatitis, and various cancers).

Withdrawal: Abrupt cessation of drug use can result in withdrawal symptoms that are themselves medical emergencies. Withdrawal from alcohol use can result in *delirium tremens* (DTs), visual and auditory hallucinations, convulsions, and other symptoms; many alcoholics must be sedated to dampen these effects. Withdrawal from cocaine and heroin can be equally unpleasant. Many abusers detoxify themselves; still others detoxify in what are called "social" detoxification programs, but there are some who must detoxify under medical supervision.

Drug Toxicity (Overdose): Finally, some drug abusers die from intentional or accidental drug overdoses. A sufficiently large quantity of alcohol will cause acute alcohol poisoning and occasionally death. Based on results with laboratory animals, the ratio of lethal to effective doses of marijuana is on the order of thousands to one, and so it would be practically impossible to smoke enough marijuana to cause one's death. The lethal dose of heroin, however, is dangerously close to the effective dose. Most deaths from drug overdose prove to be unintentional; they result from users consuming purer samples of drugs than they are used to or from contaminants introduced as pure drugs are "cut" for sale. (Thus, one compelling argument for regulated legalization of such substances is that the purity and dosages could be controlled.)

The Indirect Health Effects of Drug Use

The behavioral correlates of substance abuse are often as damaging to health as the direct somatic effects:

Trauma: Much trauma arises from substance abuse: injury and death that result from driving under the influence of intoxicants, from bar fights and other assaults, from house fires accidentally set by cigarette smokers, from homicides and suicides where alcohol and other drugs are implicated, even from gun shot wounds to bystanders caught between rival drug gangs.

Sexually Transmitted Disease: Throughout the rest of the industrialized world, gonorrhea, syphilis, and chancroid have nearly disappeared, but these diseases have "been increasing at epidemic rates among urban minority populations in the U.S." (Aral and Holmes, 1991: 62). Gonorrhea and syphilis rates have risen sharply among blacks since the middle 1980s; the gap between black and white rates has been increasing. Chancroid, rare since World War II, has resurfaced in a number of major urban outbreaks dating to 1984. The inner-city sexually transmitted disease (STD) epidemic has been further characterized by the emergence of drug-resistant bacterial strains and the rapid spread of incurable viral STDs--HIV most notably, but also various types of herpes and human papillomavirus as well. These trends, while not confined to the central city minority poverty population, are overwhelmingly most evident in that context.

What accounts for this epidemic? "Recent studies in urban areas [...] have found that transmission of gonorrhea, syphilis, chancroid and HIV infections has been closely associated with the exchange of sex for drugs such as crack. Women, particularly adolescent women, sometimes engage in very large numbers of sexual contacts to support their addiction" (Aral and Holmes, 1991: 68). (The same can also be said of some young men.)

The effects of the STD epidemic on the inner city public health system have been quite consequential. Aral and Holmes surveyed 23 public STD clinics throughout the U.S.; 19 reported that their clinics were closing earlier than in the past, that patients had to wait longer to receive care, or that increased numbers were simply being turned away because of inadequate treatment resources.

Auto Immune Deficiency Syndrome (AIDS)

Among the diseases transmittable through sexual contact, none is more fearsome than AIDS. The two principal vectors for the transmission of the virus that

73

causes AIDS are sexual contact with infected persons and sharing syringes with infected addicts. Owing to widespread adoption of "safe sex" practices, the rate of new AIDS cases among male homosexuals has begun to decline; in turn, the rate of new cases involving heterosexual transmission and sharing of infected drug paraphernalia has increased. Much of the heterosexual transmission of HIV involves the exchange of sex for drugs or for money to buy drugs; obviously, all of the HIV cases secondary to the use of infected syringes are drug-related. Thus, more and more, AIDS has come to be seen as a drug-related disease.

AIDS is also a costly disease, costs increasingly borne by the public sector. The cost of medical care for an AIDS patient averages $40,000 to $75,000 between diagnosis and death, which is about $5,000 per month during the clinically active phase of the HIV infection. Data on financing of AIDS care in Los Angeles, San Francisco, and New York from 1983 to 1988 show a striking increase in the share paid through Medicaid and a precipitous decline in the share paid by private insurance (Green and Arno, 1990). Thus, the financial burden of caring for AIDS victims has been shifted to the public sector.

With no cure in sight, our best weapon against AIDS is prevention; this means "safe sex" and "clean needles." Taking these up separately:

Clean Needles: Drug abusers do not get HIV because they use intravenous drugs but because they share needles with infected persons and thereby become infected themselves. Clean, sterile syringes can be purchased for about 25 cents apiece but under current law they can only be dispensed via prescription (for example, to diabetics who must inject insulin). In contrast, the health care costs for clinically active AIDS patients is about $5,000 per month or (let us say) about $50,000 from onset to death. At a quarter apiece, $50,000 would buy 200,000 sterile syringes. If we gave drug addicts free syringes and only prevented one HIV infection per each 200,000 syringes distributed, the program would break even. Moreover, a large number of "free needle" programs have been instituted in Europe and Australia; all available evidence suggests a "success rate" vastly better than 1 in 200,000. John Daniels, former mayor of New Haven, argues that although needle exchanges are certainly no substitute for adequate drug treatment, they would at least keep people alive until they could be helped.

74

The U.S. experience with free needle programs has been highly restricted. A pathetically limited program in New York City (Anderson, 1991) was opposed by law enforcement officials and conservative politicians because it seemed to condone illicit drug use, just as free condom programs are often opposed because they seem to promote (or legitimize) promiscuity. Many health professionals opposed the program for fear that it would increase the rate of addiction. Black leaders opposed the program because they feared it would become a substitute for adequate anti-drug education and treatment; the black churches were opposed because the very notion of free needles was offensive to conventional morality. The limited program that was eventually enacted was possible only because it was disguised as a clinical trial on the effectiveness of needle exchanges in slowing the spread of HIV infection. The effectiveness of such programs has, of course, been demonstrated in a number of cities elsewhere in the world where free needle programs are already the norm, and as a matter of fact several U.S. cities, among them Chicago, Tacoma, San Francisco, and others, have begun to follow suit in the past few years (Des Jarlais and Friedman, 1994).

Many observers found a darker motive in the intense opposition to the New York experiment. One addict remarked, "This talk about addicts liking to share needles is a lie. They don't want to give out free needles because they want us to die, and they see it [AIDS] as a good way to get rid of us" (Anderson, 1991: 1510). This addict has a good point. Yolanda Serrano has asked, "What do we do, just let them die and take their families with them?" Apparently, our collective answer to this blunt question is "Yes." It appears that we would prefer to let HIV infection spread among the drug-using population and shoulder the ensuing costs of treating the infection, rather than do something cheap and effective to arrest the spread of the disease in the first place.

Safe Sex: The spread of HIV through sexual contact is less amenable to cheap solutions. As indicated, the rate of new HIV cases among male homosexuals has begun to decline because of safe sex practices. Bisexual and heterosexual transmission is, however, on the increase; for the most part, this means that infected males transmit the disease to their female partners. (Transmission from infected females to males is relatively rare since the sexual act involves a much larger transfer of male body fluids to women than of female body fluids to men). Thus, increasingly, HIV and AIDS have become women's health issues.

The links among women, AIDS, and drugs are found principally in prostitution by young women to support their drug habits. Condoms are moderately effective preventatives, but prostitutes are rarely in a position to insist on condom use. Even male partners in consensual unions frequently resist condoms because of comfort or cultural values. So while it would be as easy and cheap to supply prostitutes (or anybody else) with free condoms as to supply IV drug abusers with needles, there is not much reason to suppose that doing so would slow the spread of the HIV virus. Short of a vast reduction in the demand for drugs, the only viable solution is to lower the cost of drugs so that young women are not required to prostitute themselves to obtain drugs, and this speaks to issues of decriminalization and legalization taken up in the concluding chapter.

There is nothing about the use of drugs *per se* that gives people HIV infections. The link between drugs and AIDS is the exchange of sex for drugs or the use of infected syringes. Our present policies needlessly worsen both problems.

Crack Cocaine and the Public Health Care System

There are only about 850,000 regular crack users in the U.S., but there is reason to believe that crack use is concentrated among inner-city poor people who rely for health care on the public health system (free clinics, public hospitals, and Medicaid). There is evidence that crack has begun to overwhelm that system.

Central city clinics now expect large numbers of drug abusers among their patients. Retrospective chart review for patients in an inner-city Detroit clinic found evidence of drug and alcohol abuse in more than half (Cahill and Hodgkins, 1991). The largest group of abusers (45%) were poly-substance-abusive (that is, used multiple drugs in combination); another third were cocaine-only or heroin-only abusers; only 22% were strict alcoholics. Abusers, especially men, had more frequent visits than non-abusers and were also more likely to present with chronic physical disorders. "This differential pattern of clinic use, wherein relatively young male substance abusers constitute a significant part of the clientele, accentuates the unusual burden that a clinic of this type faces" (1991: 1013). Resources spent on treating the diseases and disorders of substance abusive patients are therefore not available for prenatal care, child immunization, tuberculosis screening, or other worthwhile things.

76

Part of the problem is that there are few alcohol and drug treatment options open to indigent persons. If we were more effective in treating substance abuse, we could worry less about (and spend less on) treating the health consequences. Treatment for substance abuse is not generally covered by Medicaid, the mechanism that funds most indigent health care (General Accounting Office, 1992). Detoxification is covered only if provided under medical supervision in a hospital setting; social detoxification and most "room and board" non-medical approaches, as well as long-term residentially based treatment programs, are excluded under Medicaid payment guidelines. Only some private health care plans cover treatment for alcohol and drug dependency and usually restrict treatment to a single 28-day intervention. There is practically no evidence that alcohol and drug disorders can be "cured" with a one-shot, one-month program.

Summary

Cigarettes and alcohol cause much morbidity and mortality; the abuse of illegal substances also has negative health consequences although they are fairly trivial in comparison and stem more from the behaviors associated with drug use than from the effects of drugs themselves. Thus, drug use is responsible for a nation-wide epidemic of sexually transmitted disease because large numbers of young addicts (both male and female) engage in large numbers of sexual encounters to support their habits. Most of these STDs are curable; AIDS is not. AIDS is also transmitted through sharing of infected syringes, a mode of transmission that could be interrupted with free needle programs.

In addition to effects on the health of individuals, widespread drug use in the inner cities has begun to overwhelm the public health system. As more health care for drug-related illnesses is shifted to the public sector, a concern arises about the quality of care drug users and their families receive. The drug problem has exacerbated the problems inherent in our two-tiered system of health care: a first tier financed through private insurance for the affluent, white, and unaddicted; a second tier financed through the public sector for the non-affluent, nonwhite, and substance abusive--separate, unequal, and ultimately tragic.

Eight

Drugs and Drug Treatment

Introduction

Each year, about two million Americans enter treatment for alcohol or drug problems. Many critics argue that a rational approach would involve providing treatment options to millions more. Would expanded treatment for alcohol and drug dependencies contribute significantly to solving America's drug problem?

Whether more treatment would help solve the drug problem depends largely on whether substance abuse treatment is effective in "curing" the disorder, and this is far more complex than most people realize. It is not the sort of question that admits of a simple yes or no answer. What do we mean by alcohol and drug treatment? Which kinds (or modalities) of treatment are we to consider? How much treatment is necessary to provide the cure?

Treatment modalities for substance abuse range from methadone maintenance for heroin addicts to acupuncture to a range of more traditional individual and group psychodynamic and behavioral therapies. Different kinds of treatment are used for different kinds of addicts and for different kinds of drugs; approaches that may be effective in some contexts may prove wholly ineffective in others. There is a related question of "dosage," namely, how much of any particular treatment, administered at what frequency or intensity, and for what duration, is necessary to overcome alcohol or drug dependencies? Is "treatment" best thought of as a one-time intervention or as a continuous, on-going effort.

Further, what does it mean to say that treatment is "effective?" What goal should treatment achieve? Is abstinence the only acceptable outcome? Or is treatment effective if it leads to a reduction, but not cessation, of drug use? If the latter, then how large a reduction would be required to consider treatment a success? For how long? If we define success as permanent, life-long abstinence from all substances, then failure will be the norm. If we accept some temporary reduction in drug use as a success, then there will be fewer failures.

78

Perhaps "success" has less to do with reduced consumption than with associated behavioral aberrations. If we "treat" crack addicts by giving them vocational training and finding them jobs so that they can support their addiction through work rather than crime, should that be considered a success? Alternatively, is it enough to make abusers abstinent, or does "success" also imply something about peoples' enhanced capacity to hold jobs, be productive, maintain personal relationships, avoid criminal activity, and the like? If the net result is clean and sober criminals, has treatment accomplished anything worthwhile?

Even assuming that a given treatment modality is "effective," is it equally effective for all types of abusers? Or does effective treatment require matching specific interventions or strategies to different client characteristics and needs? Should we expect an alcohol treatment program that works well with business executives and professionals to work equally well with homeless alcoholics or with the chronically mentally ill? How do environmental barriers or facilitators interact with treatment to produce outcomes? Can success be achieved just by treating abusers, or does the environment have to be "treated" as well?

Raising questions about effectiveness also raises questions about relative costs and benefits. Even if we can show that a particular treatment is effective for a particular class of abusers, are the successes large enough to justify the investment? How much success of what sort is necessary to offset costs?

Much of the "research" on the effectiveness of substance abuse treatment is essentially anecdotal or impressionistic; relatively few randomized, controlled clinical trials have been undertaken; issues of comparison, conceptualization, and measurement are always problematic. Thus, the research literature is by no means definitive.

There is tremendous diversity within and between major alcohol and drug treatment modalities. To illustrate, methadone maintenance programs for heroin addicts vary enormously in the frequency and dosage of methadone administered, in the kinds of drug counselling offered to addicts, in the presence or absence of ancillary interventions such as job counselling, stress management, educational programs, etc., and in dozens of other ways. Any one program represents a unique cluster of diverse programmatic elements, services, and interventions;

comparisons across programs are difficult or impossible. Even when it can be shown that a program "works," it is often unclear which treatment elements are responsible for the program's success.

Here we discuss only the major modalities of treatment currently available in the U.S. Among the approaches not discussed are traditional individual and group psychotherapy, behavioral modification, cognitive therapy, family therapy, psychopharmacological therapies other than methadone maintenance, religious milieu therapy, and acupuncture. Proponents of each of these approaches claim high rates of success, but there is little or no reliable scientific evidence to support such claims, certainly none to suggest that any "alternative" treatment is more effective than the mainstream approaches.

Major Modalities of Substance Abuse Treatment

Detoxification: "Detoxification is therapeutically supervised withdrawal [from alcohol or drugs] to abstinence over a short term, that is, up to 21 days but usually 5 to 7 days, often using pharmacological agents to reduce discomfort or the likelihood of medical complications" (Gerstein and Harwood, 1990: 16). Detoxification means "sobering up" or "drying out." Given its short term and limited impact, many clinicians and researchers do not consider detoxification to constitute treatment *per se*; it is, rather, a necessary prerequisite to treatment. By itself, detoxification rarely produces recovery from alcohol or drug dependence; multiple detoxification episodes usually do not lead to recovery either. Still, detoxification represents the most commonly employed substance abuse intervention, accounting for an estimated 100,000 hospital admissions annually (Gerstein and Harwood, 1990: 16).

Medical detoxification is a short-term (usually 5 to 7 day) hospital-based intervention whose principal aim is to eliminate physiological dependence on alcohol or opiates in a controlled, safe setting. Typically, withdrawal from the drug of abuse is managed by administering other drugs. Recently, residentially-based *social* detoxification programs have emerged as a less costly "sobering up" alternative for abusers who do not need medical supervision (which turns out to be most abusers). Either form of detoxification is apparently effective in successful management of withdrawal itself, but neither is especially effective in

80

"curing" abuse. Relapse (resumption of alcohol or drug use) is on the order of 95% or more and multiple detoxification episodes are common (De Leon, 1990). In the absence of other follow-on interventions, detoxification is largely ineffective as a treatment (see Newman, 1979; Gerstein and Harwood, 1990).

Methadone Maintenance: Prior to 1923, when the government banned drug therapy for withdrawal from opiates, morphine was the predominant therapeutic intervention for heroin addiction in the U.S. From 1923 until 1935 addiction treatment was generally unavailable. In 1935, the U.S. Public Health Service opened a facility in Lexington, Kentucky; a similar facility was opened in Fort Worth, Texas, in 1938. Both were essentially prison hospitals, although both also accepted non-criminal addicts on a volunteer basis. These were the only addiction treatment programs available until the mid-1950s, when New York's Riverside Hospital opened its addiction detoxification facility. Soon, other hospital-based programs were opened elsewhere in New York City. All of these programs consisted of detoxification from opiates without drug therapy; early studies showed relapse rates on the order of 90% or worse (Vaillant, 1973).

The failure of these early psychotherapeutic treatment modalities was largely attributed to the physical and psychological effects of opiate withdrawal and the inability of psychotherapy to stem users' persistent cravings for the drug (Gerstein and Harwood, 1990; Lowinson *et al.*, 1992). Marie Nyswander (1956), an early pioneer in methadone treatment, concluded that "a careful search of the literature failed to disclose a single report in which withdrawal of drug and psychotherapy had enabled a significant fraction of the patients to return to the community and live as normal individuals." The realization that traditional interventions had failed, coupled with an increase in heroin usage during the 1950s (much of it in New York City), prompted medical and legal experts to question the wisdom of federal policies based on prevention and criminalization and to seek to reestablish controlled distribution of narcotics as a legal therapy for the management of opiate withdrawal.

Methadone hydrochloride is a synthetic narcotic first developed in Germany toward the end of the Second World War and used experimentally at the Lexington facility and elsewhere in the early 1960s in a series of experiments on withdrawal from opiates. It was first approved for treatment of heroin and other opioid dependencies in the U.S. by the Food & Drug Administration (FDA) in 1972. Until 1985, when naltrexone hydrochloride gained FDA approval, it was the only drug approved for such treatment. Methadone remains the modal treatment for opiate addiction. As of the early 1990s, about 200,000 persons were in methadone treatment world-wide, half in the U.S.

Methadone "cures" opiate addiction only in the limited sense that it has physiological effects similar to opioids and therefore satisfies the addict's cravings, making withdrawal and abstinence more easily managed. Initially, methadone was used in *lieu* of morphine only to assist withdrawal; once withdrawal had been accomplished, other therapies could be employed to sustain abstinence. Only later was methadone used for maintenance of addicts as well.

Early research showed that methadone had several advantages over morphine in managing withdrawal. Unlike morphine, methadone does not produce mood swings or a drug "high." Thus, normal daily functioning is not impaired. In addition, an adequate, once-daily methadone dose of 80-120 milligrams produces a pharmacological cross-tolerance that effectively blocks the narcotic effects of heroin. Thus, the methadone-maintained heroin-user cannot get "high" from ingesting heroin. Furthermore, methadone is safe, non-toxic, and has minimal side effects (Isbell, 1948; Isbell and Vogel, 1949; Lowinson *et al.*, 1992).

Since methadone treatment replaces one drug with another, it remains controversial. Nonetheless, it has been far more widely and soundly analyzed than any other drug intervention (see De Leon, 1990; Gerstein and Harwood, 1990; Lowinson *et al.*, 1992; Hubbard, 1992). Several conclusions emerge:

(1) Without long-term methadone maintenance at adequate dose levels, most heroin abusers are not able to maintain participation in associated psychotherapeutic interventions.

(2) While methadone maintenance often results in marked reduction or complete cessation of heroin use, many clients (sometimes a majority) continue to abuse other drugs such as crack and alcohol.

(3) Methadone maintenance is successful only if addicts can be retained in their program; without retention, the large majority relapse. Retention and relapse are inversely related; to be effective, methadone maintenance must be continued more or less indefinitely.

(4) When methadone-maintained addicts relapse, other secondary positive outcomes such as lessened criminal activity, lowered transmission of HIV, enhanced employment, and higher social functioning also decline.

(5) The Treatment Outcome Prospective Study (TOPS), one of three federally sponsored, large-scale, multi-site studies of drug treatment programs, showed that methadone maintenance is a cost-effective treatment. If one considers only the treatment-related increase in employment and earnings of former addicts, the evidence suggests basic parity between program costs and benefits; if reductions in criminal activity are also factored in, the ratio of benefits to costs is dramatically positive (Harwood *et al.*, 1988).

(6) Time in treatment (retention) is the most significant factor affecting treatment outcomes (Ball and Ross, 1991). (This is true of all treatment modalities.) While retention is affected by numerous factors, research has repeatedly confirmed that continued dose-appropriate methadone maintenance results in higher treatment retention and therefore enhances treatment efficacy; likewise, a leading factor in attrition from treatment is inadequate dose levels.

Despite its proven effectiveness and relatively low cost, methadone maintenance is not a panacea for addiction to heroin and other opiates. A recent report from the Institute of Medicine concludes that even assuming an improved nation-wide network of clinics providing adequate methadone doses to all who request treatment, we "might realistically be capable of reaching and dramatically accelerating the recovery of one-third of all those who become dependent on heroin" (Gerstein and Harwood, 1990: 154). Thus, methadone maintenance might solve only a third of the heroin problem.

Therapeutic Communities (TCs): The term "therapeutic community" refers to a broad range of residential programs exhibiting tremendous diversity in the populations served, drug or drugs abused, length of stay, types of staff, etc. TCs developed out of the Synanon experience and initially tended to enroll opiate abusers. Over time, however, TCs have responded to other types of users and drugs. A recent study of 15 TCs and more than 1100 clients conducted for NIDA reported crack cocaine to be the major drug problem now treated in TC-style programs (O'Brien and Biase, 1992).

Despite many differences, TCs share a number of critical elements and a basic orienting philosophy:

"The TC views drug abuse as a deviant behavior, reflecting impeded personality development and deficits in social, educational, and economic skills. Its antecedents may lie in socio-economic disadvantage, poor family effectiveness and in psychological factors. In this perspective, substance abuse is a disorder of the whole person. Addiction is a symptom, not the essence of a disorder. The problem is not the drug but the person" (De Leon, 1990: 119).

"Physiological dependency is secondary to the wide range of influences which control individual's drug use behavior. Invariably, problems and situations associated with discomfort become regular signals for resorting to drug use (...)

"In the TC's view of recovery, the aim of rehabilitation is global (...) The primary psychological goal is to change the negative patterns of behavior, thinking, and feeling that predispose drug use; the main social goal is to develop a responsible drug free lifestyle. Stable recovery, however, depends upon a successful integration of these social and psychological goals" (De Leon, 1986: 7-8, as quoted in Gerstein and Harwood, 1990: 155).

TCs are holistic in orientation and seek a variety of outcomes beyond abstinence or reduced drug usage. They tend to be highly structured with a mix of individual and group psychotherapy; have clear rules and expectations regarding behavior, systems of punishment, and rewards; and attempt to resocialize the self over a relatively long period of time (typically ranging from 6 to 24 months).

Given their diversity, TC approaches are difficult to evaluate. As Gerstein and Harwood (1990: 156) note, "conclusions about the effectiveness of TCs are limited by the difficulties of applying standard clinical trial methodologies to a

84

complex, dynamic treatment milieu." Thus, it is not surprising that there is diversity of opinion regarding their effectiveness. Some claim success rates as high as 85%. However, these figures prove largely meaningless: they often result from selection biases (i.e., discarding most failures before calculating success), or from the absence of control group comparisons, or from basing the measure of success on a very few clients who are successfully retained in treatment for extended periods.

An analysis of the fourteen TCs included in TOPS (Hubbard *et al.*, 1989) showed substantial improvement among clients who remained in treatment for the full regimen. Evidence from the Drug Abuse Reporting Program (DARP, an earlier federally sponsored multi-site, multi-treatment assessment; see Simpson *et al.*, 1979), a study of graduates and dropouts from New York's Phoenix House Program (De Leon *et al.*, 1982), and our own assessment of over 670 homeless substance abusers in the New Orleans Homeless Substance Abusers project (Wright, Devine and Joyner, 1993) found much the same. In addition, studies find that the large majority of TC clients "end virtually all illicit drug taking and other criminal behavior while they are in residence" (Gerstein and Harwood 1990: 182), a limited but not insubstantial benefit. There is a fairly substantial literature showing that TC approaches can be effective in at least some cases. A number of these studies also document enhanced social adjustment, psychological improvement, and reduced criminality among TC residents (De Leon, 1990; Wright, Devine and Joyner, 1993).

The "bad news" is that TC effectiveness is highly dependent on retention in treatment. In general, positive outcomes are observed only among clients who complete the full treatment regimen; persons who leave treatment prematurely generally do not show significant or lasting benefits. Unfortunately, premature "splitting" is the norm; "typically, about 15 percent [of TC admissions] will graduate after a continuous stay" (Gerstein and Harwood, 1990: 189). Thus, the inability of most TC programs to retain clients for more than a month or two is a significant barrier; "the minimum retention necessary to yield improvements in long-term outcomes seems to be several months" (Gerstein and Harwood, 1990: 189). Therapeutic communities apparently work well for a minority of drug abusers, but they are no panacea.

Short-Term Residential Chemical Dependency Treatment (CD):   There are a number of similarities between therapeutic communities and a variety of short-term (usually 28-day) residentially based chemical dependency treatment programs (sometimes called "Minnesota" or "Hazelden" programs).   Both types typically employ Twelve Step models (see below), take a holistic, disease-oriented, educational approach to the problem of chemical dependency, and view substance abuse as stemming from multiple psychological and sociological causes.   In addition, both initially emerged to treat alcoholism but have increasingly come to treat other types of chemical dependencies.

Still, CD programs typically differ from TC programs in a number of respects. CD programs are shorter (usually lasting only 28 days *vs*. 6 or more months), are one-shot treatment events (with more emphasis on post-treatment "self-help" and less emphasis on formal, post-treatment aftercare), are often hospital-based or affiliated, and tend to be more hierarchical and staff-directed with a higher proportion of credentialed, professional staff.   In recent years, these programs have become the predominant model for privately-financed chemical dependency treatment.   Thus, the demographic profile of CD clients shows a more affluent, educated, and employed client base than that enjoyed by other approaches.

Residential CD programs of the sort we are describing have existed since the late 1940s (Anderson, 1981) but have been less extensively studied than a number of other approaches (Gerstein and Harwood, 1990: 172; Geller, 1992: 461).   Much of the "evidence" concerning their effectiveness comes from in-house clinicians and researchers.   Even this literature confirms that the CD approach is more effective in treating alcoholics than in treating other kinds of drug abusers; and even among alcoholics treated in CD settings, only 30% to 50% achieve as much as a year's abstinence from alcohol--that is, if the in-house studies are to be believed.   A randomized clinical trial conducted in Finland found that only 14% of CD clients were still abstinent from alcohol one year later (Geller, 1992: 461). Thus, relapse varies between half and 85%.   And here too, retention in treatment is a critical variable; relapse is even higher among those who fail to complete the full treatment regimen.   Relatively little is known about the factors that condition retention (whether in CD or other treatment approaches), but initial client motivation is assumed to be most important.

Twelve Step Self-Help Groups: Alcoholics Anonymous (AA), Narcotics Anonymous (NA), Cocaine Anonymous (CA), Drugs Anonymous (DA):   Alcoholics Anonymous (AA) originated in the 1930s and was the first of the Twelve Step programs. By the mid-1960s, AA was estimated to have over 170,000 members organized in thousands of AA groups.   Survey evidence indicates that historically, AA membership consisted predominantly of white, middle-class, married males (Bean, 1975). AA has become much more diverse and over the past quarter century, a variety of other Twelve Step programs have developed to meet the needs of other substance abusers. These other Twelve Step programs exhibit even more demographic diversity among their members.

The influence of the Twelve Step approach is ubiquitous throughout the substance abuse treatment industry. As Nace (1992: 486) correctly notes, "it would be difficult today to find a substance abuse treatment program that does not espouse the principles of AA."

Twelve Step self-help programs eschew the professional-client relationship and are based instead on a highly spiritualized fellowship model where the substance abuser learns and works the Twelve Steps "one a day at a time" with the support of other members. New members are expected to obtain a sponsor, that is, a more established and knowledgeable member who has attained an extended period of sobriety, but the emphasis is always on self-help and a singular spiritual commitment to the Twelve Steps, which are as follows:

The Twelve Steps of Alcoholics Anonymous

1. We admitted we were powerless over alcohol and that our lives had become unmanageable.

2. Came to believe that a Power greater than ourselves could restore us to sanity.

3. Made a decision to turn our will and our lives over to the care of God as we understood him.

4. Made a searching and fearless moral inventory of ourselves.

5. Admitted to God, to ourselves, and to another human being the exact nature of our wrongs.

6. We were entirely ready to have God remove all these defects of character.

7. Humbly asked Him to remove our shortcomings.

8. Made a list of all persons we had harmed and became willing to make amends to them all.

9. Made direct amends to such people wherever possible, except when to do so would injure them or others.

10. Continued to take personal inventory and when we were wrong promptly admitted it.

11. Sought through prayer and meditation to improve our conscious contact with God as we understood Him, praying only for knowledge of His will for us and the power to carry that out.

12. Having had a spiritual awakening as the result of these Steps, we tried to carry this message to alcoholics, and to practice these principles in all our affairs.

(From Alcoholics Anonymous World Services, Inc., 1978)

Over the years, numerous efforts have been made to analyze Twelve Step programs. There is substantial anecdotal evidence that continued involvement in Twelve Step programs facilitates abstinence and other positive outcomes (social adjustment, increased sense of well-being). Moreover, the Twelve Steps are widely used in conjunction with other treatment modalities due mainly to their directive behavioral orientation and their apparent success in overcoming denial.

Again, in-house studies have claimed success rates on the order of 80% to 90%, but there is little real evidence to substantiate such claims. Emrick's (1987) review of a number of studies of Twelve Step programs suggests that 50% to 60% of *active* AA members manage at least one year of continuous sobriety, but individuals who "fall off the wagon" are far more likely to discontinue active AA involvement, thereby inflating the measure of success. There are no randomized clinical trials of Twelve Step approaches, partly because of the general hostility of AA-type programs to research. Thus, De Leon (1990: 126) concludes that "the effectiveness of twelve-step-oriented self-help groups has not been sufficiently documented to meet conventional scientific standards, largely because of client self-selection factors and the philosophical disinclination of these groups to undergo rigorous evaluation."

Summary

Alcohol and drug treatment programs represent a considerable expense and almost all discussions of "what to do about drugs" argue for an expansion of treatment services as a critical component of an overall solution. Still, it is clear that *the effectiveness of alcohol and drug treatment has been oversold.* The best one can conclude is that some types of treatment seem to work for some people some of the time; no treatment or intervention has been shown to work well for most people most of the time. Relapse is the most common response to all alcohol and drug interventions.

Throughout the research literature and across treatment modalities, retention in treatment is found to constitute the most significant barrier to effectiveness. We would suggest that retention is mostly a function of entering motivation, not of specific program characteristics; the principal barriers to recovery are social, psychological, and behavioral--not pharmacological. If the motivation to change is strong, all treatments work equally well, and if motivation is weak or non-existent, then no treatment works well. In short, no therapeutic intervention has been shown to work consistently for unmotivated clients.

Relapse rates for all approaches are usually on the order of two-thirds to three-quarters in the first year. We conclude that effective "treatment" must come from within the substance-abusive person, not from externally imposed treatment approaches. In this sense, there is no such thing as alcohol and drug treatment. The best treatment can accomplish is to assist motivated abusers to seize control of their lives and addictions.

89

The predominance of Twelve Step thinking in the treatment industry has caused many to believe that once people are addicted, they are somehow addicted for life, that there is no such thing as a "cure" for chemical dependencies. As Fingarette (1988) and others have pointed out, many people prove able to overcome any kind of addiction, *assuming they are motivated to do so.* In general, the most severe cases of addiction are also those most likely to come under treatment, which accounts in substantial part for the high relapse rate.

Again owing to AA influence, we are accustomed to looking on addiction as a disease in the same way that hypertension or tuberculosis are diseases. The "disease model" of addiction has accomplished much good but it has also caused some harm in that it basically denies that people can take personal responsibility for their own actions and behaviors. The disease model encourages a mind-set that addicts are "sick" and therefore require a "cure" as opposed to the more accurate view that addicts are engaged in self-destructive patterns of behavior and need to stop it. The essential difference between a disease such as tuberculosis and the disease of addiction is that one cannot cure tuberculosis with an exercise of will or responsibility. In the absence of will and responsibility, no treatment has been shown to be effective.

There is little evidence that any drug or alcohol treatment is especially effective. Most clients show some improvement while in treatment but subsequent relapse is very high; it is also well-known that many chemically dependent persons improve on their own without treatment (spontaneous remission). It has yet to be shown that any form of treatment systematically improves on the rate of spontaneous remission (Gerstein and Harwood, 1990; Akers, 1992). If this is correct, then substance abuse treatment can at best facilitate recovery among persons who are already motivated to recover, not "cause" recovery among persons who are not. In turn, motivating abusers and addicts to stop using drugs will require social and economic conditions in which sobriety is clearly preferable to intoxication, and these are not the conditions faced by the addicts and abusers who have stimulated the War on Drugs. There are many reasons to promote more widely available alcohol and drug treatment options, among them the fact that nothing undermines motivation quite so quickly as being told that there is a six-month wait to enter treatment. But in and of itself, more treatment will not solve America's "drug problem."

Nine

Drugs: What Is the Solution?

Introduction: The War on Drugs

Between the early 1980s and the present, annual spending on the War on Drugs grew from about $1 billion to $12 billion (Horgan, 1993); many new laws such as the Department of Defense Authorization Act of 1982, The Comprehensive Crime Control Act of 1984, The Anti-Drug Abuse Act of 1986, The Anti-Drug Abuse Act of 1988, and the Crime Control Act of 1990 were enacted to strengthen and extend the nation's drug prohibition policy (BJS, 1992: Ch. 3).

The regulatory mechanisms embodied in these anti-drug laws are wide-ranging: tougher sentencing for drug offenses (including mandatory sentencing and the redefinition of some offenses as capital crimes), expanded police powers of search and surveillance, new or enhanced prosecutorial weapons (for example, the Racketeer Influenced and Corrupt Organization [RICO] law, provisions for seizure of assets and pretrial detention), mandatory urine analysis for specific populations and work groups, legislative authority for military assistance in support of drug law enforcement (including equipment, training, intelligence gathering, investigation, and interdiction), and the creation of the Office of National Drug Control Policy (ONDCP), whose director is charged with coordinating all national drug control efforts. The War on Drugs now involves a "total offensive" on both the domestic and international fronts.

What has this new "get tough" policy accomplished? By some criteria, the pay-off has been handsome: the number of arrests for drug offenses has increased (so sharply that our jail and prison facilities are barely able to accommodate the growing numbers), the tonnage of drugs destroyed or interdicted has grown (see below), and more drug-related assets have been seized (in 1990 alone, DEA property seizures amounted to a billion dollars; see BJS, 1992: 156).

Perhaps the most visible "success" of the War on Drugs has been the increasing tonnage of illegal drugs seized by DEA and other law enforcement agencies and removed from the domestic market. From 1982 to 1989, cocaine seizures grew twelve-fold, from less than 12,000 pounds to 155,000 pounds; heroin seizures more than quintupled; seizures of illicit or illegally diverted prescription stimulants climbed from several million to almost 150,000,000 dose units per year (BJS, 1991: 464). Bulk marijuana seizures declined from about 3 million pounds in 1982 to less than 800,000 pounds in 1989, but DEA efforts on the marijuana front were being redirected away from the foreign crop and more towards domestic cultivation. Eradication of domestic marijuana escalated from 2.5 million plants destroyed in 25 states in 1982 to 130 million plants destroyed in 49 states in 1989 (BJS, 1992: 150). During these same years, DEA seizures of clandestine drug laboratories increased from around 200 to 800 labs per year (BJS, 1991: 467).

What do these impressive numbers really mean about the illicit drug supply? Even highly optimistic assessments conclude that no more than about 30% of drugs bound for the U.S. market are intercepted (Staley, 1992; Wisotsky, 1990; Reuter and Kleinman, 1986). While the confiscated tonnage has definitely increased, according to the State Department's March 1991 "International Narcotics Control Strategy Report," world production of marijuana, coca, and opium has also increased by at least 73%, 16%, and 53% respectively between 1987 and 1991 (BJS, 1992: 36). The more we destroy, the more they grow. As a result, the net effect of our interdiction, destruction and drug seizure policies on the supply of illegal drugs to the U.S. market has been trivial.

In addition, producers and traffickers have proven quite adept at shifting their operations to respond to law enforcement efforts. A highly-touted multi-agency crackdown on drug trafficking in Miami in the 1980s resulted in substantial drug seizures, but the industry responded by shifting importation to New Orleans, to other Gulf Coast gateways, and to the Mexican border. The drug industry has been quite adaptive in other ways. Traffickers have learned to use smaller, faster boats and to substitute planes for boats where possible. They have repackaged the product in smaller, more easily concealable lots in *lieu* of bulk cargo. And, like all other entrepreneurs, drug traffickers have invested in new product development, for example, crack cocaine (easily concealable and affordable, as opposed to marijuana, very bulky, or powdered cocaine, very expensive).

These adaptations have allowed traffickers to continue despite every effort by DEA and other agencies. The net result of our supply-side efforts is that the street prices of marijuana, cocaine, and heroin have remained relatively stable during the past decade and have even declined in some areas (Staley, 1992: 197-99; BJS, 1992: 54). In short, illicit drugs remain readily available. The declining use of illegal drugs chronicled in the NHSDA surveys (Chapter 2) and in NIDA's surveys of high school seniors (Johnston, O'Malley, and Bachman, 1991) has resulted mostly from changing attitudes about drugs (which may well signal some degree of success in the demand-reduction efforts of the War on Drugs), not from any significant decline in availability or accessibility.

Drug prohibition as practiced for the last decade has been much-ballyhooed but expensive failure. We have not been able to reduce the supply nor diminish demand enough to make a difference, and we cannot arrest enough dealers or users to alter the situation significantly. On the other hand, as Kaplan (1983), Nadelmann (1989), Staley (1992) and others have pointed out, our prohibitionist policies have put immense strains on the criminal justice system, provided ample opportunities for corruption and racketeering, and undermined the rule of law by fostering widespread predatory criminal activity.

Public Opinion

Despite widespread frustration with the War on Drugs, most Americans continue to oppose the alternative, decriminalization or controlled legalization of currently illegal drugs. A 1990 Gallup poll asked: "Some people feel that current drug laws haven't worked and that drugs like marijuana, cocaine, and heroin should be legalized and subject to government taxation and regulation like alcohol and tobacco. Do you think legalization is a good idea or a bad idea?" A large majority, 80%, considered legalization a bad idea, and only 14% considered it a good idea (Colasanto, 1990). The 1989 Survey of High School Seniors (Johnston *et al.*, 1991) found that only 17% of the students favored making marijuana use legal, exactly half the percentage of a dozen years earlier. An additional 19% felt that marijuana use should be treated as a misdemeanor much as a parking ticket; half felt that marijuana use should remain criminal.

Polls indicate that the American public supports expanded efforts in drug education and demand reduction (BJS, 1992: Ch. 2); many also show that most Americans oppose legalization and support even further expansion of efforts to restrict supply. Most also favor even harsher criminal penalties for drug sales, possession, and use. The public voice says "get tougher."

But just how much "tougher," realistically, can we get? "Getting tough" has not been successful in the past (consider Prohibition), is clearly unsuccessful in the present, and is not likely to be any more successful in the future. Thus, many have concluded that the policies being pursued to fight the drug problem may in fact be making things worse, not better. Thus, decriminalization or controlled legalization is being more seriously considered as an alternative.

The Case For Decriminalization or Controlled Legalization

Arguments in favor of decriminalization or legalization are not monolithic and arise from diverse proponents across the ideological spectrum. Some favor outright, unrestricted legalization of all illicit drugs (at least among adults), while others favor a more limited policy that would legalize use or possession in small amounts but not distribution or trafficking. Still others favor decriminalization or outright legalization of marijuana but not of other drugs.

The diversity of recommendations is matched by the variety of premises from which legalization is argued. In some cases, the argument is strictly moral or philosophical. Libertarians and some conservatives such as William F. Buckley (1985) and Milton Friedman (1990) argue that drug use is a privacy issue and not an appropriate concern of government policy. These *philosophes* acknowledge that drug use may not be healthy, indeed, is often reckless and self-destructive, but that people have an inalienable right to make unhealthy, reckless and self-destructive decisions about their private lives and behavior. In this framework, government drug policy is a serious and unwarranted abrogation of personal liberty by an invasive state eager to trample on the rights of private citizens.

Buckley's argument is buttressed by pragmatic considerations. He writes, "I am on record as having opposed it [legalization] in the matter of heroin. The accumulated evidence draws me away from my own opposition, on the purely

94

empirical grounds that what we now have is a drug problem plus a crime problem" (1985: 11).

Other critics argue that our present drug policy is wildly inconsistent and hypocritical. They point to the widespread tolerance (even encouragement) and legality of the use of alcohol, tobacco, and hundreds of other mind-altering and addictive licit drugs on the one hand, and our condemnation of marijuana, cocaine, or heroin use on the other. To many, this constitutes a mean-spirited double standard. It is also very hard to justify on grounds of practical merit, since the mortality, morbidity, and economic costs associated with the use of tobacco and alcohol vastly exceed those associated with all other drugs combined.

Many critics argue that a great deal of drug use and abuse is actively encouraged, tolerated, downplayed, or ignored, especially among the more affluent, while for reasons not always apparent, other drugs are condemned as illegal, their benefits denied, their risks inflated, and their users persecuted. Many believe this double standard is motivated by racism and constitutes a form of tyranny.

Others view drug use as a demand-driven social and health issue, not a criminal justice issue. Fighting drug abuse requires demand reduction through efforts that address its social and psychological roots and health consequences. Imprisoning addicts and users cannot solve the problem. Thus, current law-enforcement policies fail because they only attack symptoms, not underlying causes (see Staley, 1992; Trebach, 1987). Advocates of legalization also commonly argue that present policy is either ineffective, counter-productive, or not cost-beneficial.

The strongest and most thoughtful case in favor of expanded legalization has been argued by Ethan Nadelmann of Princeton University (1989, 1990). Nadelmann argues that we need to de-emphasize reliance on the criminal justice system as a means of dealing with the drug problem and redirect resources away from drug use *per se* and towards drug abuse, prevention, treatment, and education, including alcohol and tobacco in this redirected offensive. Nadelmann advocates the legal availability of some or all currently-illicit substances but simultaneously recommends vigorous efforts to reduce consumption by means other than criminal sanction. Moreover, he supports the transfer of government resources from anti-drug law enforcement to prevention and treatment.

Most advocates of more liberal drug policy recognize that decriminalization or legalization is no panacea. By themselves, policy changes in this direction will not solve the drug problem; moreover, there is a real risk of increased drug use and abuse as a consequence. Thus, nearly all thoughtful legalization proposals include expanded efforts in education and treatment. No one who favors controlled legalization expects magic. The expectation, rather, is of significant improvement over current conditions, for the following reasons:

• Criminal justice efforts to control drug use are inherently limited when they target supply rather than demand. So long as demand remains strong, drugs will remain available and will be used.

• Current efforts to disrupt the supply of drugs have proven ineffectual; they are readily offset by increasing production and by other market adaptations.

• Current policy foolishly conflates use with abuse, dependence, and addiction (see Chapter 5). Most drug users are casual, recreational, and self-controlled drug consumers; only a minority are in any sense abusive, drug-dependent, or addicted. The failure to distinguish between use and abuse means that we waste a lot of resources attempting to regulate, control or prevent innocuous behavior, leaving fewer resources to be spent preventing socially destructive behavior.

• Current anti-drug law enforcement efforts are both costly and ineffective; much that we consider problematic about drugs results more from our policy of drug prohibition than from drug use or abuse *per se*. Nadelmann (1989: 941) argues that "the greatest beneficiaries of the drug laws are organized and unorganized drug traffickers. The criminalization of the drug market effectively imposes a *de facto* value-added tax that is enforced and occasionally augmented by the law enforcement establishment and collected by the drug traffickers."

• Much of the multi-billion dollar illegal drug market could be recaptured in tax revenues which could then be used for education, prevention, and treatment programs. Alcohol and tobacco sales amount to about $80 billion per year; taxation of alcohol and tobacco raises more than $20 billion per year. If illegal drugs were taxed at similar rates, if the illegal drug market is in fact a $40 billion a year enterprise (see Chapter 3), and if the going price of drugs were halved as a result of decriminalization, then drug taxes would raise something on the order of $5 billion annually, which would in itself fund an approximate *doubling* of alcohol and drug treatment programs.

• Decriminalization and controlled legalization would alleviate a great deal of violence and other predatory crime, especially in the inner cities. Increased availability and reduced prices would lessen the need to resort to crime and violence to support consumption; likewise, controlled legal commerce in drugs would be highly disciplined, in contrast to the violent free-for-all that now exists.

• The health costs of illicit drug use are over-stated and represent only a small fraction of the costs of alcohol and tobacco use. It is irrational and hypocritical to designate marijuana, cocaine, or heroin as illegal when alcohol and tobacco are legal, readily available, and much more widely abused.

• A legal, regulated drug market would eliminate many of the health risks associated with the content and purity of illicit drugs and, assuming a "clean needles" program as part of the overall legalization package, would reduce the transmission of AIDS and other infections by IV drug users.

One additional argument is put forth by Staley (1992):

"Through drug prohibition, public policy has created a vast black market for illicit substances, fueling violence and disrespect for law and human life. These values become an essential element of survival in economically devastated urban areas that offer few legitimate opportunities for employment. (...) These values are reinforced by a political system that appears increasingly arbitrary as civil liberties and the respect for property are sacrificed for political expediency. Through the abrogation of personal freedoms and liberties engendered by the War on Drugs, the victims of drug prohibition learn that the arbitrary imposition of values and punishment is acceptable and encouraged. The rules governing behavior in the licit and illicit sectors of the economy become a technical, legal differentiation rather than an indication of substantive differences in conduct and behavior. (...) Drug prohibition works against the best interests of the community by dampening the incentives for its citizens to pursue economically productive and prosperous employment in the legitimate sector. Drug prohibition encourages new entrants into the labor force to emphasize short-term gains through drug-trafficking rather than the long-term gains from legitimate employment and occupational training" (Staley, 1992: 228-229).

Maintaining the Status Quo: The Case Against Legalization

There is, of course, a case to be made for current prohibitionist policies, one argued by those who oppose decriminalization or legalization of currently illicit drugs. Perhaps the strongest argument is that liberalized drug laws might substantially increase drug use, abuse, and dependence (see, for example, Inciardi, 1991). Many acknowledge that there is some merit in the arguments for decriminalization but that the costs would far exceed any of the alleged benefits. Some would argue that if decriminalization resulted in even one new addict, the price would be too high.

Many who favor the status quo also base their argument on important ethical considerations; the most common is that society should not condone or encourage drug use. Some have even claimed that advocating legalization is akin to advocating slavery in that addicts are enslaved by drugs just as Africans were enslaved by Europeans (A. M. Rosenthal, quoted in Staley, 1992: 230).

The arguments in favor of the status quo have been ably summarized by one of the architects of current drug policy, William Bennett, former drug czar and one-time Secretary of Education. Writing about the "The Legalization Debate" (see *Business Today*, Fall, 1990: 48-50), Bennett argues that the costs of legalization would be "intolerably high." His key points:

● Legalization would remove all incentive to stay away from drugs, at least in the short run.

● Expanded access to drugs would result in soaring drug use and abuse.

● High costs and the risk of punishment remain our most effective deterrents.

● Taking the profit out of the drug trade will not alter the situation because lower costs and diminished legal risk will encourage additional drug use.

• Alternatively, taxation of a legalized drug market will maintain the price of drugs at their current level (or recreate a tax-avoiding black market that would resemble the present market).

• Even if drug consumption is legalized and the price of drugs drops, street crime will not be reduced because criminals will continue to steal, thieve, rob and intimidate to pay for their other material needs and desires.

• The health problems associated with drug use would increase as the rate of use increased.

"Legalization advocates think that the cost of enforcing drug laws is too great. But the real question--the question they never ask--is what does it cost not to enforce those laws. The price that American society would have to pay would be intolerably high. We would have more drug-related accidents at work, on the highways, and in the airways. We would have even bigger losses in worker productivity. Our hospitals would be filled with drug emergencies. We would have more school kids on dope, and that means more drop-outs. More pregnant women would buy legal cocaine, and then deliver tiny, premature infants....Now, if you add to that the costs of treatment, social welfare, and insurance, you've got the price of legalization" (Bennett, 1990: 50).

Many of these arguments have merit but speak more cogently to the specific form that decriminalization would have to take than to the rationality of present policy. The risk of increased use is real, but the implication is not continued prohibition but rather enhanced efforts to educate people about the dangers of drugs. This is not as naive as it sounds (or as Bennett would have one believe). Alcohol consumption is legal for adults; that notwithstanding, strenuous efforts have been made in the last decade to educate drinkers about the risks, and consumption has in fact gone down. Likewise, legal and heavily taxed alcohol has not created a large black market in illegal, untaxed alcohol. The high costs of drugs and the risk of legal punishment are demonstrably not "effective deterrents." Many criminals who support their drug habits through crime might well continue their criminal activities for other reasons even if drugs were relatively cheap and legally available, which is only to argue that the "drug problem" and the "crime problem" are not the same problem. Arguments of the sort advanced by Bennett

99

counsel great caution in formulating a policy of decriminalization, but do not offset the evident failure of current policy or the need to think creatively and realistically about alternatives.

Charting A New Course

We conclude that a policy of limited (or regulated) legalization of drugs is necessary and desirable. The War on Drugs has failed mainly because its premises are misguided, counter-productive, or false. A rational drug policy must be organized around or consistent with the following five principles:

(1) People use drugs because they like drugs and the effects drugs create. *Per se*, drug use is a quest for pleasurable sensation or an effort to dull unpleasurable sensation, not a behavioral aberration and not fundamentally unlike a large number of other relatively risky things that people do to amuse or divert themselves. Drugs and drug abuse--of both legal and illegal substances--cause some very real problems and tragic consequences, but supply-oriented policies have exacerbated many of these problems and created still others.

(2) Society has a legitimate right and responsibility to regulate the production and distribution of drugs and insure individual and public safety. At the same time, the government's right to restrict such activities should be premised on consistency and an appreciation of equally legitimate individual privacy rights.

(3) The essential goal of drug policy should be to minimize harm to both individuals and society as a whole. The most legitimate and effective mechanisms to accomplish this are regulation of the drug market and efforts to educate people about drugs, not criminal sanctions. Effective, constructive drug policy would focus on demand reduction, education, prevention, responsible use, and substance abuse treatment rather than interdiction or punishment. (Recent evidence is quite encouraging in these respects [Chapter 2]. Use of all drugs has declined substantially over the past decade as people have become more aware of the associated health risks.)

(4) Demand creates it own supply (sometimes called the first principle of micro-economics). So long as people want drugs or seek the pleasures that drugs

provide, there will be profit in providing drugs and therefore, they will be provided. The only realistic policy decision is whether to encourage and abet a vast, illegal narcotics empire as the provider, as we presently do, or whether to allow legal provision under strict regulatory controls and, not incidentally, government taxation of the product. Even acknowledging the strong and obvious downside to controlled legalization, it at least has some chance of success as a policy, which present policies do not.

(5) The myths of addiction that undergird much current thinking about drugs must be confronted and rejected. The relevant evidence is very clear: while many people, especially during their younger years, experiment with some drugs, most often alcohol, tobacco, and marijuana, very few actually "graduate" to harder drugs such as cocaine or heroin; most who do experiment with the harder drugs come to use them casually and recreationally, not addictively; finally, drug use is something that most people grow out of as they mature. Some users of all substances do eventually develop dependencies and addictions, but they represent only a small fraction of the total drug-consuming population.

Present policy is often premised on hyperbole. In overstating the magnitude of the problem, in lumping together such diverse substances as marijuana and heroin as if they were one and the same (or as if use of the former necessarily leads to use of the latter), while tolerating the far greater costs associated with excessive alcohol and tobacco consumption, we have undermined our moral authority to educate people about the very real risks associated with drug use and abuse.

We acknowledge a strong downside to any policy of legalization. However, the compensating benefits more than offset these costs. Moreover, the probable increase in use, abuse, and addiction can be offset to some extent by expanded education focussing on the realistic hazards and risks of drugs (including alcohol and tobacco), by programs to encourage responsible drug use, by regulation of the product, by aggressive enforcement of distribution laws, and by providing treatment to anyone who needs and desires it, regardless of ability to pay.

Given the evidence on the effectiveness of treatment (Chapter 8), our recommendation to provide treatment on demand may seem pointless. However, treatment is highly effective if initial motivation is strong. Moreover, there is every reason to believe that on-going research and experimentation will discover methods to increase motivation, to enhance treatment effectiveness, and to match clients with treatment modalities more efficiently. Research has already made it obvious that effective treatment rarely involves a single intervention; usually, multiple or continuous efforts are required.

Without proper motivation, no treatment for alcohol and drug disorders can be effective. One should not conclude from this observation that treatment is meaningless, but rather that no motivated individual should be denied treatment because a treatment slot or fee source is unavailable. Even more fundamentally, we need to foster conditions and opportunities that keep people from wanting to use drugs in the first place, that make sobriety preferable to inebriation. Sadly, this is not the case for many of our nation's people. The desire to change one's behavior, to defer immediate gratification for longer-term objectives, necessarily requires a meaningful future; lacking that meaningful future, "Just Say No" is a pointless admonition. Drugs will always be a seductive alternative to people whose futures are without meaning, opportunity, and dignity. Drug prohibition does not and cannot alter this inescapable fact. Decriminalization and controlled legalization will not "solve" the drug problem, but they are steps in a sensible direction.

References

Akers RL. 1992. *Drugs, Alcohol, and Society*. Belmont, CA: Wadsworth.

Alcoholics Anonymous. *Twelve Steps and Twelve Traditions*. New York: AA World Services, 1978.

Anderson DJ. 1981. *Perspectives on Treatment: The Minnesota Experience*. Center City, MN: Hazelden.

Anderson KM, WP Casteeli, D Levy. 1987. Cholesterol and Mortality: 30 Years of Followup From the Framingham Study. *Journal of the American Medical Association* 257: 2176-2180.

Anderson W. 1991. The New York Needle Trial: The Politics of Public Health in the Age of AIDS. *American Journal of Public Health* 81 (11, November): 1506-1517.

Anglin MD, Y Hser. 1987. Addicted Women and Crime. *Criminology* 25: 359-97.

Anglin MD, G Speckart. 1988. Narcotics Use and Crime: A Multisample, Multimethod Analysis. *Criminology* 26: 197-233.

Aral SO, KK Holmes. 1991. Sexually Transmitted Diseases in the AIDS Era. *Scientific American* 264(2): 62-69.

Ball JC, A Ross. 1991. *The Effectiveness of Methadone Maintenance Treatment*. New York: Springer-Verlag.

Bean MH. 1975. Alcoholics Anonymous: AA. *Psychiatry Annals* 5(2): 3-64.

Bennett W. 1990. The Legalization Debate. *Business Today* (Fall): 48, 50.

Bluestone B, B Harrison. 1986. *The Great American Job Machine: The Proliferation of Low Wage Employment in the U.S. Economy*. Washington, DC: Joint Economic Commission, U.S. Congress.

Bradbury K, A Downs, K Small. 1982. *Urban Decline and the Future of American Cities*. Washington, DC: Brookings.

Brecher EM and the Editors of Consumer Reports. 1972. *Licit and Illicit Drugs*. Mount Vernon, NY: Consumers Union.

Buckley W. 1985. Legalize Dope. *The Washington Post* (April 1): A-11.

Bureau of Justice Statistics, U.S. Department of Justice. 1988. *Drunk Driving*. Special Report (February).

Bureau of Justice Statistics, U.S. Department of Justice. 1991. *Sourcebook of Criminal Justice Statistics, 1990*, NCJ-130580 (September).

Bureau of Justice Statistics, U.S. Department of Justice. 1992. *Drugs, Crime, and the Justice System: A National Report from the Bureau of Justice Statistics*, NCJ-133652 (December).

Bureau of Justice Statistics, U.S. Department of Justice. 1993. *Drugs and Crime Facts, 1992*, NCJ-139561 (March).

Cahill DF, BJ Hodgkins. 1991. The Urban Health Care Clinic and Its Substance Abuse Population. *Medical Care* 29 (10, October): 1004-1016.

Clark KB. 1965. *Dark Ghetto: Dilemmas of Social Power*. New York: Harper.

Colasanto D. 1990. Widespread Public Opposition to Drug Legalization. *The Gallup Poll Monthly* 292 (January): 2-8. Princeton, NJ: The Gallup Poll.

Collins JJ. 1986. The Relationship of Problem Drinking to Individual Offending Sequences. Pp.89-120 in A Blumstein, J Cohen, J Roth, CA Visher (eds.), *Criminal Careers and 'Career Criminals,'* vol. 2. Washington, DC: National Academy Press.

Curra J. 1994. *Understanding Social Deviance: From the Near Side to the Outer Limits*. New York: Harper Collins.

Currie E. 1985. *Confronting Crime: An American Challenge*. New York: Pantheon.

De Leon G. 1986. The Therapeutic Community for Substance Abuse: Perspective and Approach. Pp. 5-18 in G. De Leon and JT. Ziegenfuss, Jr. (eds.), *Therapeutic Communities For Addictions*. Springfield, IL: Charles C. Thomas.

De Leon G. 1990. Treatment Strategies. Pp. 115-138 in JA Inciardi (ed.), *Handbook of Drug Control in the United States*. New York: Greenwood Press.

De Leon G., HK Wexler, and N Jainchill. 1982. The Therapeutic Community: Success and Improvement Rates 5 Years After Treatment. *The International Journal of the Addictions* 17(4): 703-747.

Des Jarlais DC, SR Friedman. 1994. AIDS and the Use of Injected Drugs. *Scientific American* 270:2 (February): 82-88.

Devine JA, JD Wright. 1993. *The Greatest of Evils: Urban Poverty and the American Underclass*. Hawthorne, NY: Aldine de Gruyter.

Emrick C. 1987. Alcoholics Anonymous: Affiliation Processes and Effectiveness as Treatment. *Alcoholism* (NY) 11: 416-423.

Englehart P, H Robinson, HD Carpenter. 1992. The Workplace. Pp. 1034-1048 in JH Lowinson, P Ruiz, RB Millman (eds.), *Substance Abuse: A Comprehensive Textbook*, 2nd ed., Baltimore, MD: Williams and Wilkins.

Fagan J. 1990. Social Processes of Delinquency and Drug Use Among Urban Gangs. Pp. 183-219 in CR Huff (ed.), *Gangs in America*. Newbury Park, CA: Sage.

Famularo R, K Stone, R Barnum, R Wharton. 1986. Alcoholism and Severe Child Maltreatment. *American Journal of Orthopsychiatry* 56: 481-485.

Faupel CE, CB Klockars. 1987. Drug-Crime Connections: Elaborations From the Life Histories of Hard-Core Heroin Addicts. *Social Problems* 34: 54-68.

Fingarette H. 1988. Alcoholism: The Mythical Disease. *The Public Interest* 91 (Spring): 3-22.

Fisk N. 1984. Epidemiology of Alcohol Abuse and Alcoholism. *Alcohol Health and Research World*, 9 (1, Fall): 4-7.

Friedman M. 1990. An Open Letter to Bill Bennett. Pp. 114-16 in D Boaz (ed.), *The Crisis in Drug Prohibition*. Washington, DC: Cato Institute.

Geller A. 1992. Rehabilitation Programs and Halfway Houses. Pp.458-466 in JH Lowinson, P Ruiz, RB Millman (eds.), *Substance Abuse: A Comprehensive Textbook*, 2nd ed., Baltimore, MD: Williams and Wilkins.

General Accounting Office. 1992. *Substance Abuse Treatment: Medicaid Allows Some Services But Generally Limits Coverage*. Washington, DC: USGAO.

Gerstein DR, HJ Harwood (eds.). 1990. *Treating Drug Problems*, volume 1. Washington, DC: National Academy Press.

Goodwin DW. 1992. Alcohol: Clinical Aspects. Pp. 144-151 in JH Lowinson, P Ruiz, RB Millman (eds.), *Substance Abuse: A Comprehensive Textbook*, 2nd ed., Baltimore, MD: Williams and Wilkins.

Goodwin DW, JB Crane, SB Guze. 1971. Felons Who Drink. *Quarterly Journal of Studies in Alcohol* 32: 136-147.

Green J, PS Arno. 1990. The 'Medicaidization' of AIDS: Trends in the Financing of HIV-Related Medical Care. *Journal of the American Medical Association* 264: 1261-1266.

Grinspoon L, JB Bakalar. 1992. Marijuana. Pp. 236-246 in JH Lowinson, P Ruiz, RB Millman (eds.), *Substance Abuse: A Comprehensive Textbook*, 2nd ed., Baltimore, MD: Williams and Wilkins.

Harwood HJ, RL Hubbard, JJ Collins, JV Rachal. 1988. The Costs of Crime and the Benefits of Drug Abuse Treatment: A Cost-Benefit Analysis Using TOPS Data. Pp. 209-235 in CG Leukefeld and FM Tims (eds.), *Compulsory Treatment of Drug Abuse: Research and Clinical Practice*. NIDA Research Monograph 86, Rockville, MD: NIDA.

Horgan J. 1990. Test Negative. *Scientific American* (March): 18, 22.

Horgan J. 1993. A Kinder War. *Scientific American* (July): 24, 26.

Hubbard RL. 1992. Evaluation and Treatment Outcome. Pp. 596-611 in JH Lowinson, P Ruiz, RB Millman (eds.), *Substance Abuse: A Comprehensive Textbook*, 2nd ed., Baltimore, MD: Williams and Wilkins.

Hubbard RL, ME Marsden, JV Rachal, HJ Harwood, ER Cavanaugh, HM Ginsburg. 1989. *Drug Abuse Treatment: A National Study of Effectiveness*. Chapel Hill, NC: University of North Carolina Press.

Huizinga DH, S Menard, DS Elliott. 1989. Delinquency and Drug Use: Temporal and Developmental Patterns. *Justice Quarterly* 6 (September): 419-55.

Inciardi JA. 1986. *The War on Drugs*. Palo Alto, CA: Mayfield.

Inciardi JA (ed.). 1990. *Handbook of Drug Control in the United States*. New York: Greenwood Press.

Inciardi JA (ed.). 1991. *The Drug Legalization Debate*. Newbury Park, CA: Sage.

Isbell H. 1948. Methods and Results of Studying Experimental Human Addiction to the Newer Synthetic Analgesics. *Annals of the New York Academy of Science* 51: 108.

Isbell H, V Vogel. 1949. The Addiction Liability of Methadone (...) and its Use in the Treatment of the Morphine Abstinence Syndrome. *American Journal of Psychiatry* 105: 909.

Jarvik ME, NG Schneider. 1992. Nicotine. Pp. 334-356 in JH Lowinson, P Ruiz, RB Millman (eds.), *Substance Abuse: A Comprehensive Textbook*, 2nd ed., Baltimore, MD: Williams and Wilkins.

Johnson BJ, PJ Goldstein, E Preble, J Schimeidler, D Lipton, B Spunt, T Miller. 1985. *Taking Care of Business: The Economics of Crime By Heroin Abusers*. Lexington, MA: DC Heath.

Johnston LD, PM O'Malley, JG Bachman. 1991. *Drug Use Among American High School Seniors, College Students and Young Adults, 1975-1990*, volume 1, High School Seniors. DHHS Publication (ADM) 91-1813. Washington, DC: NIDA.

Johnston LD, PM O'Malley, LK Eveland. 1978. Drugs and Delinquency: A Search for Causal Connections. Pp. 137-56 in D Kandel (ed.), *Longitudinal Research on Drug Use*. Washington, DC: Hemisphere Press.

Jones KL, DW Smith, CM Ulleland. 1973. Patterns of Malformation in Offspring of Chronic Alcohol Mothers. *Lancet* 1: 1267-1271.

Kaplan J. 1983. *The Hardest Drug: Heroin and Social Policy*. Chicago: University of Chicago Press.

Kasarda J. 1985. Urban Change and Minority Opportunities. Pp. 33-67 in P Peterson (ed.), *The New Urban Reality*. Washington, DC: Brookings.

Kinney J, G Leaton. 1992. *Understanding Alcohol*, 2nd ed. St. Louis: Mosby Year Book.

Kirk-Othmer. 1983. Stimulants. Pp. 747-761 in *Kirk-Othmer Encyclopedia of Chemical Technology*, vol. 21, 3rd ed. New York: John Wiley & Sons.

Leonard KE, T Jacob. 1988. Alcohol, Alcoholism and Family Violence. Pp. 383-406 in VB Van Hasselt *et al.* (eds.), *Handbook of Family Violence*. New York: Plenum.

Levine C, NN Dubler. 1990. Uncertain Risks and Bitter Realities: The Reproductive Choices of HIV-Infected Women. *Milbank Quarterly* 68: 3.

Lillie-Blanton M, JC Anthony, CR Schuster. 1993. Probing the Meaning of Racial/Ethnic Group Comparisons in Crack Cocaine Smoking. *Journal of the American Medical Association* 269 (24 February): 993-997.

Lowinson JH, IJ Marion, H Joseph, VP Dole. 1992. Methadone Maintenance. Pp. 550-561 in JH Lowinson, P Ruiz, RB Millman (eds.), *Substance Abuse: A Comprehensive Textbook*, 2nd ed. Baltimore, MD: Williams and Wilkins.

Lowinson JH, P Ruiz, RB Millman (eds.), *Substance Abuse: A Comprehensive Textbook*, 2nd ed. Baltimore, MD: Williams and Wilkins.

Martz L. 1990. A Dirty Drug Secret. *Newsweek* (February 19): 74, 77.

Massing M. 1992. What Ever Happened to the War on Drugs? *The New York Review of Books* 39 (June 11): 42-46.

McNagny SE, RM Parker. 1992. High Prevalence of Recent Cocaine Use and the Unreliability of Patient Self-Report in an Inner-City Walk-In Clinic. *Journal of the American Medical Association* 267 (26 February): 1106-1108.

Mills CW. 1959. *The Sociological Imagination*. New York: Oxford University Press.

Moore R, F Malitz. 1986. Underdiagnosis of Alcoholism By Residents in an Ambulatory Medical Practice. *Journal of Medical Education* 61 (January): 46-52.

Morgan JP. 1988. The 'Scientific' Justification For Urine Drug Testing. *University of Kansas Law Review* 36: 683-697.

Murdoch D, RO Pihl, D Ross. 1990. Alcohol and Crimes of Violence: Present Issues. *International Journal of the Addictions* 25:1065-1081.

Musto D. 1987. *The American Disease: Origins of Narcotics Control.* New York: Oxford University Press.

Nace EP. 1992. Alcoholics Anonymous. Pp. 486-495 in JH Lowinson, P Ruiz, RB Millman (eds.), *Substance Abuse: A Comprehensive Textbook*, 2nd ed. Baltimore, MD: Williams and Wilkins.

Nadelmann EA. 1989. Drug Prohibition in the United States: Costs, Consequences, and Alternatives. *Science* 245 (September 1): 939-947.

Nadelmaann EA. 1990. The Legalization Debate. *Business Today* (Fall): 49, 51.

National Institute on Alcohol Abuse and Alcoholism. 1987. *Alcohol and Health: Sixth Special Report to the U.S. Congress from the Secretary of Health and Human Services.* Rockville, MD: NIAAA.

National Institute on Alcohol Abuse and Alcoholism. 1990. *Alcohol and Health: Seventh Special Report to the U.S. Congress from the Secretary of Health and Human Services.* Rockville, MD: NIAAA.

National Institute on Drug Abuse. 1991a. *National Household Survey on Drug Abuse: Main Findings 1990.* Rockville, MD: NIDA.

National Institute on Drug Abuse. 1991b. *National Household Survey on Drug Abuse: Population Estimates 1991.* Rockville, MD: NIDA.

National Institute on Drug Abuse, National Institute on Alcohol Abuse and Alcoholism. 1991. *National Drug and Alcoholism Treatment Unit Survey (NDATUS): 1989 Main Findings Report.* Rockville, MD: NIDA and NIAAA.

Newman R. 1979. Detoxification Treatment For Narcotics Addicts. Pp. 21-29 in R Dupont, A Goldstein, J O'Donnell (eds.), *Handbook on Drug Abuse*, Rockville, MD: NIDA.

Norris J, LA Cubbins. 1992. Dating, Drinking, and Rape: Effects of Victim's and Assailant's Alcohol Consumption on Judgements of Their Behavior and Traits. *Psychology of Women Quarterly* 16: 179-191.

Nurco DN, TW Kinlock, TE Hanlon. 1990. The Drugs-Crime Connection. Pp. 71-90 in JA Inciardi (ed.), *Handbook of Drug Control in the United States*. New York: Greenwood Press.

Nyswander ME. 1956. *The Drug Addict As a Patient*. New York: Grune and Stratton.

O'Brien WB, DV Biase. 1992. Therapeutic Community (TC): A Coming of Age. Pp. 446-457 in JH Lowinson, P Ruiz, RB Millman (eds.), *Substance Abuse: A Comprehensive Textbook*, 2nd ed. Baltimore, MD: Williams and Wilkins.

Office of National Drug Control Policy Office (ONDCP). 1991. *What America's Users Spend on Illegal Drugs*, Technical Paper (June). Washington, DC: ONDCP.

Pernanan K. 1991. *Alcohol in Human Violence*. New York: Guilford Press.

Primm BJ. 1992. Future Outlook: Treatment Improvement. Pp. 612-626 in JH Lowinson, P Ruiz, RB Millman (eds.), *Substance Abuse: A Comprehensive Textbook*, 2nd ed. Baltimore, MD: Williams and Wilkins.

Reuter P, M Kleinman. 1986. Risks and Prices: An Economic Analysis of Drug Enforcement. Pp. 289-340 in M Tonry, N Morris (eds.), *Crime and Justice: An Annual Review of Research*, vol. 7. Chicago: University of Chicago Press.

Rice DP, S Kelman, LS Miller. 1991. Estimates of Economic Costs of Alcohol and Drug Abuse and Mental Illness, 1985 and 1988. *Public Health Reports* 106 (3, May-June): 280-292.

The Robert Wood Johnson Foundation. 1992. *Substance Abuse: Annual Report-1992*. Princeton, NJ: The Robert Wood Johnson Foundation.

Rovner, S. 1993. Young Adult's Drug Use May Be on the Upswing. *New Orleans Times Picayune* (Associated Press), August 29: D-6.

Simpson DD, LJ Savage, MR Lloyd. 1979. Follow-Up Evaluation of Treatment of Drug Abuse During 1969 to 1972. *Archives of General Psychiatry* 36: 772-780.

Sheley JF, JD Wright, MD Smith. 1993. *Firearms, Violence, and Inner-City Youth.* Draft report submitted to the National Institute of Justice and Office of Juvenile Justice and Delinquency Prevention. Department of Sociology, Tulane University.

Shuckit MA. 1989. *Drug and Alcohol Abuse*, 3rd ed. New York: Plenum.

Smith JD. 1987. Measuring the Informal Economy. *Annals of the American Academy of Political and Social Science* 493 (September): 83-99.

Staley S. 1992. *Drug Policy and the Decline of American Cities*. New Brunswick, NJ: Transaction Publishers.

Trager O (ed). 1986. *Drugs in America: Crisis or Hysteria?* New York: Facts on File.

Trebach A. 1987. *The Great Drug War*. New York: Macmillan.

Turner TB, VL Bennett, H Hernandez. 1981. The Beneficial Side of Moderate Alcohol Use. *Johns Hopkins Medical Journal* 148: 53.

U.S. Bureau of the Census. 1990. *1987 Census of Manufactures: Industry Series/Beverages*. Washington, DC: USGPO.

U.S. Bureau of the Census. 1992. *Statistical Abstract of the United States, 1992*. Washington, DC: USGPO.

Vaillant, GE. 1973. A 20 Year Follow-Up of New York Narcotic Addicts. *Archives of General Psychiatry* 29: 237-241.

Weil A. 1972. *The Natural Mind: A New Way of Looking at Drugs and the Higher Consciousness*. Boston: Houghton Mifflin.

The White House. 1992. *National Drug Control Strategy Budget Summary* (January). Washington, DC: The White House.

111

Wilson WJ. 1987. *The Truly Disadvantaged*. Chicago: University of Chicago Press.

Winick C. 1992. Epidemiology of Alcohol and Drug Abuse. Pp. 15-29 in JH Lowinson, P Ruiz, RB Millman (eds.), *Substance Abuse: A Comprehensive Textbook*, 2nd ed. Baltimore, MD: Williams and Wilkins.

Wisotsky S. 1990. *Beyond the War on Drugs*. Buffalo, NY: Prometheus Books.

Witte AD. 1986. The Underground Economy in the United States and Western Europe. Pp. 204-229 in RW Lindholm (ed.), *Examination of Basic Weaknesses of Income As the Major Federal Tax Base*. New York: Praeger.

Wright JD, 1989. *Address Unknown: The Homeless in America*. Hawthorne, NY: Aldine de Gruyter.

Wright JD, 1991. *Project Cincinnati: The Volunteers of America's Community and Neighborhood Drug Offensive and its Impact on Young People In Cincinnati*. Cincinnati, OH: River Valley VOA (October).

Wright JD, JA Devine, LM Joyner. 1993. *The Least of Mine: The New Orleans Homeless Substance Abusers Project, Final Report*. Department of Sociology, Tulane University (August).

Wright JD, PH Rossi, 1986. *Armed and Considered Dangerous*. Hawthorne, NY: Aldine de Gruyter.

Wright JD, E Weber, 1987. *Homelessness and Health*. Washington: McGraw Hill.